Rekindle Virginia

Rekindle Virginia

The Flames of Revival

Compiled by
DOROTHY "DOT" DALTON

Rekindle Virginia

The Flames of Revival

© 2021 Dorothy "Dot" Dalton

All rights reserved. No portion of this book may be reproduced, stored in a retrieval system, or transmitted in any form or by any means—electronic, mechanical, photocopy, recording, scanning, or other—except for brief quotations in critical reviews or articles, without the prior written permission of the publisher.

ISBN 9780578816814 paperback
ISBN 9780578966670 ebook
Library of Congress Control Number: 2021912819

Cover Concept by:
Tom Powell
tom@theaddisongroup.com

Cover and Interior Design by:
Chris Treccani
www.3dogcreative.net

Preface

This book is a miracle.

First of all, let me say that I am not a writer, and I hated history in school because I felt it was just the memorization of a lot of dates. I'm also not a Bible teacher or minister of the gospel, but I am a follower of Jesus Christ and He is my Savior and Lord. So the record is straight, I'm a networker and a major project organizer with the giftings God has given me. My deceased husband, Clem, was the history lover in the family who read history books every night. Maybe the importance of history might have rubbed off on me.

After being a widow and very active in several ministry and community projects, I had several major surgeries. God had sidelined me to the point I had, like Paul, to learn to be content. I had resigned everything.

Earlier for over 20 years, we had been onsite praying and interceding for revival; in my Jerusalem, Suffolk; and my Judea, the State of Virginia; and my Samaria, our Nation. Then the burden ceased. All I could do was ask why Lord.

After seven years, and early in 2019, God started stirring my spirit again. My original dreams and vision of bringing together the Body of Christ, His Church, into unity for revival, was rebirthed in a new way. I was given a new appreciation of the importance of the state of Virginia, and for God's original plan to reach the Native Americans with the gospel of Jesus Christ. God chose England and the Anglican church to bring the gospel to America as part of His Kingdom's purposes. England was part of the Protestant Reformation that had spread all over Europe.

Virginia is God's "Eastern Gate" to America for God's Kingdom on earth's Christian plan. Not Plymouth which came 13 years later. God used King James I of England, who signed The First Virginia Charter of 1606 authored by Rev. Richard Hakluyt, and the Anglican Church to establish Virginia. I feel we need to honor the Anglican Church of England for bringing Jesus to America, for it was responsible for planting the cross of Jesus at Cape Henry and dedicating this land for the spreading of His gospel to this nation and to the whole world. Also for starting the first Protestant church service on America's soil at Jamestown, the first convert to Christianity, first representative type of government, etc. Virginia is certainly the Cradle and Birth place of this nation in God's heart.

After much research and reading, I found that many Protestant denominations in Virginia had Great Awakening revivals between 1740 and 1790. This was the Second Great Awakening in America after New England's Awaking with Jonathan Edwards. Virginia's ground has already been plowed, seeds of revival planted, flames of revival already have been lit. He did it once, He can do it again. Pray and Believe!!!

My prayer is that churches would use this compiled data as a teaching tool of their church's early history. Also raise up a prayer ministry in each church to believe and prepare for revival. Then unite with other churches in your area, and together believe for revival. A Third Great Awakening in America.

Acknowledgments

Many Thanks to….
My longtime spiritual mentor Dr. Raymond W. Stiles
Special friend and sister Chief G. Anne Richardson
Adopted granddaughter Anna Marshall finding books, editing, organizing, and day by day sharing
Tom Powell graphic and media vision
Robert Taylor for his love of Francis Asbury and his message
Jessica Turner for digitizing many graphs and images

A short video is also available called "Rekindle Virginia." Go to the web site www.rekindleva.com for more information, and to search for others in your area to unite in prayer by zip codes.

Dorothy "Dot" Dalton
Suffolk, Virginia
2020

Revive Us Again

Wilt thou not revive us again: that thy people may rejoice in thee? Psa. 85:6
Thine, O LORD, is the greatness, and the power, and the glory, and the victory, and the majesty. 1 Chr. 29:11

1. We praise Thee, O God! For the Son of Thy love,
2. We praise Thee, O God! For Thy Spirit of light,
3. All glory and praise To the Lamb that was slain,
4. All glory and praise To the God of all grace,
5. Revive us again; Fill each heart with Thy love;

For Jesus Who died, And is now gone above.
Who hath shown us our Savior, And scattered our night.
Who hath borne all our sins, And hath cleansed every stain.
Who hast brought us, and sought us, And guided our ways.
May each soul be rekindled With fire from above.

Refrain

Hallelujah! Thine the glory. Hallelujah! Amen.

Hallelujah! Thine the glory. Revive us again.

WORDS William P. Mackay, 1863. MUSIC John J. Husband, 1815. Public Domain.

Table of Contents

Preface	v
Acknowledgments	vii
Table of Contents	ix
Illustrations	xiii

PART I	**Europe**		**1**
	INTRODUCTION		3
	WHAT WAS GOING ON IN EUROPE		5
	PROTESTANTISM IN ENGLAND		7
		King Henry VIII	7
		King James I	7
		Protestant Reformation	8
		Martin Luther	8
		Founding of Lutherans	9
		Founding of the Church of England	9
		Founding of Puritans	10
		Founding of Quakers	11
		Reformers	12
		Ulrich Zwingli	12
		Jeanne d'Albret	13
		John Knox	13
		Theodorus Frelinghuysen	13
		Founding of Presbyterians	14
		Founding of Methodists	15
		Founding of Baptists	16
		Timeline - Protestant Reformation	17
PART II	**Early America**		**19**
	BACKGROUND		21
		Colonization Attempts by England in America	21
		King James I of England 1566 - 1625	22

	THE FIRST CHARTER OF VIRGINIA	23
	Anglican Rev. Richard Hachluit (also spelled Hakluyt)	23
	The First Charter of Virginia, April 10, 1606	24
	Purpose	28
	Land Area 1606 - 1621	29
	FIRST NATION PEOPLE, NATIVE AMERICANS	31
	What They Believed	31
	Guardians of the Land	31
	The Principal Portion Of The Territory Ruled By Powhatan	34
PART III	Establishment of Protestant	35
	Churches in Virginia	35
	ESTABLISHMENT OF PROTESTANT CHURCHES IN VIRGINIA	37
	1606 Charter under Church of England	37
	London Company First to come to Virginia (Jamestown 1607)	37
	1606 - 1621	37
	Planting the Cross at Cape Henry	38
	Anglican Rev. Robert Hunt Prayer	39
	Virginia Early History by Date	39
	Timeline - Early Protestant Denominations Churches in Virginia	42
	CHURCH OF ENGLAND	43
	First Protestant Church Service	43
	First Convert	45
	First Marriage	46
	First Thanksgiving	47
	First Representative Government Convened	48
	James Fort	49
	Maps of Early Anglican Parishes	50
	PURITANS, "INDEPENDENTS"	53
	Early Puritans	53
	Puritans in Virginia	56
	QUAKERS	59
	Early Quakers "Friends"	59
	LUTHERANS	63
	EARLY PRESBYTERIANS IN VIRGINIA (REFORMERS)	65
	BAPTISTS	67
	Early Baptists in Virginia	67
	David Barrow	70
	METHODISTS	73

John Wesley	73
Charles Wesley	76
George Whitefield (Whitfield)	77
Whitefield Took Seven Trips to America	78
George Whitefield on Slavery	81
On the Death of the Rev. George Whitefield, 1770	82
Francis Asbury	84
Maps Show Examples of Asbury Visits in Virginia	87
OTHER VIRGINIA METHODISTS	**89**
Reverend Robert Williams	89
Bishop William McKendree	91
Timeline - Early Methodists	93
METHODIST AND VIRGINIA NATIVE AMERICANS TODAY	**95**
CONTINUED INFLUENCE (VIRGINIA TRIBES)	**97**
Nansemond Indian Tribe	97
Rappahannock Indian Tribe	98
Chief G. Anne Richardson's Story	98

PART IV Great Awakening in Virginia 1740-1790 — 101

GREAT AWAKENINGS IN VIRGINIA	**103**
Overview	103
Timeline - Revivals in America	103
German Reformers and Dutch Reformers (Mennonite)	104
Presbyterian	105
Church of England (Anglican)	107
Anglican Reverend Devereux Jarratt (1732 to 1801)	108
Methodist	111
Baptist (Separatist)	113
CAMP MEETINGS	**115**
Quotes from the Great Awakening of Virginia Revivals	117
Results of the Great Awakening in Virginia, 1740 to 1790	118

PART V Rekindling the Flames of Revival — 121

REKINDLE THE FLAMES OF REVIVAL	**123**
THE BODY OF CHRIST	**125**
As Individuals	125
As a Collective Church and Region	126
A Call to Prayer and Fasting for the State of Virginia	129
Virginia Has Been Called:	129

Mission: Rekindle Flames of Revival in Virginia	131
Proposed Actions:	131
About the hymn "Revive Us Again"	132
References	133
About Dorothy "Dot" L. Dalton	135

Illustrations

Hymn - Revive Us Again	viii
Timeline - What Was Going on in Europe	6
Henry VIII	7
King James I	7
Martin Luther, Wittenberg	8
The Book of Common Prayer, 1549	9
Oliver Cromwell	10
George Fox, Quaker	11
"The Presence in the Midst" by James Doyle Penrose	11
John Calvin, Geneva	12
Ulrich Zwingli	12
Jeanne d'Albret	13
John Knox	13
Theodorus Frelinghuysen	13
Count Nikolaus von Zinzendorf	13
John Knox	14
John and Charles Wesley	15
John Wesley Preaching On His Father's Tomb	16
Timeline - Protestant Reformation in Europe	17
King James I	22
Reverend Richard Hachluit	23
Map of Virginia at the Time of the First Charter of Virginia, April 10, 1606	27
Map of Virginia at the Time of the First Charter of Virginia, London Company and Plymouth Company	29
Chief Anne Richardson	31
Virginia Algonquian Population Estimates, 17th Century	33
The Principal Portion of the Territory Ruled by Powhatan	34
The Landing at Cape Henry, April 1607	38
Reverend Hunt, First Protestant Minister	39
Virginia Early History by Date	39
Virginia Settlement and Colonies	40

Map of Virginia Counties	41
Timeline - Early Protestant Denominations Churches in Virginia	42
"First Church Service" by Scottie Marshall	44
Baptism of Pocahontas, Picture from US Capitol Rotunda	45
The Wedding of Pocahontas with John Rolfe, Lithograph by Geo Spohni, c. 1867	46
"First Thanksgiving," Sidney King	47
"First Virginia Assembly," Sydney King	48
"James Fort," Sydney King	49
Maps of Early Anglican Parishes, from "Colonial Churches of Tidewater Virginia" by George Carrington Mason, 1945	50
"Brave New World"	53
George Fox	59
"Early Quaker's Meeting Houses" Karla Smith	61
The Lutheran Church in Virginia 171-1962	63
Map of Lutheran Congregations	64
Francis Makemie	65
Samuel Davis	66
The Dunking of David Barrow and Edward Mintz	68
Map Early Churches in Virginia by Samuel Lewis	70
John Wesley	73
Seekers of the Spirit	75
Charles Wesley	76
George Whitefield	77
Benjamin Franklin	78
Phillis Wheatley	82
Francis Asbury	84
Bishop Richard Allen	86
Francis Asbury on Horseback	86
Places Visited by Francis Asbury	87
Asbury's Journey to the South	87
Robert Williams	89
Bishop William McKendree	91
Timeline - Early Methodists	93
Nansemond Indian Tribe	97
Indiana United Methodist Church	97
Indiana Methodist Church 1850, and school 1890	97
Chief Anne Richardson	98
Rappahannock Tribal Center Today	99-100
Timeline – Revivals in America	103

Map of Early German Reformers and Dutch Reformers Revivals in Virginia	104
Samuel Davis	105
Map of Early Presbyterian Revivals in Virginia	106
Profile of Devereux Jarratt, Encyclopedia Virginia	108
Map of Early Anglican Revival in Virginia	109
Map of Early Methodist Revivals in Virginia	112
Map of Early Baptist Revivals in Virginia	114
Camp Meetings	115
Timeline - Great Awakening in Virginia	120

PART I

Europe

"I will remember the deeds of the Lord;
yes, I will remember your miracles of long ago.
I will meditate on all your works and consider all your mighty deeds."

PSALM 77:11-12

INTRODUCTION

God had a plan for bringing the gospel to the New World called America. Having established the first permanent settlement at Jamestown, England was God's choice to bring the gospel of Jesus Christ to the guardians of His creation, the Native Americans, the First inhabitants of America.

God gave the vision for New World colonization to Rev. Richard Hakluyt, an Anglican Priest. Hakluyt had the vision for over 30 years, beginning during the reign of Queen Elizabeth. Hakluyt had studied maps, travel explorations, navigation, and put together the most comprehensive information on the land called Virginia. A prolific writer, he wrote "Discourse Concerning Western Planting in 1583," an eloquent plea for the English settlement in America. He prepared the public for action on "Western Planting". However, his vision was shelved after Queen Elizabeth's death.

Then came King James VI of Scotland, a Presbyterian of extremely strict upbringing, who became King James I of England. His land, which included Scotland and Ireland, led to the forming of Great Britain. King James I signed Hakluyt's "The First Charter of Virginia" on April 10, 1606. God's plan continued.

God told the Israelites to always remember His mighty deeds and to tell their children for generations to come. This holds true for His followers today. REMEMBER.

WHAT WAS GOING ON IN EUROPE

In 1380, Wyclif supervised the first complete English Bible translation. In 1456, Gutenberg published the first printed Bible in Latin, in Mainz, Germany. The Sixteenth Century was defined by great intellectualism, cultural pioneers like Leonardo da Vinci and Michelangelo, universities like the University of Paris and Wittenberg University, travel exploration, discoveries by Galileo, and writers like Shakespeare. Columbus first voyaged to the Americas in 1492. And in 1525, Tyndale's New Testament was published. During this period, the Medieval Catholic Church was in control, having come through the Middle Ages.

Turmoil also defined this era, with three great powers, England, Spain, and France, forming a European Rivalry.

- Spain's first conquest of the New World was credited to the discovery of Columbus under orders of Ferdinand and Queen Isabella, with a grant from the Pope of the Catholic Church. He visited Southern North America and called it Florida.
- France commissioned Verrazano to explore the St. Lawrence River area and called the country Canada, which then expanded west and south.
- England claimed the whole continent by the discovery of Cabot and called it Virginia. Later Sir Walter Raleigh established a Protestant Colony in the New World at Roanoke Island.

Queen Elizabeth of England was a staunch Protestant. Philip II King of Spain was Catholic with the intention of exterminating Protestantism. Henry III was King of France and Catholic, where there was a religious war between the Huguenots and Catholics. Germany was caught up in the Thirty Years' War. And Holland was in a war for independence from Spain.

Note. Overview from "The Conquest of Virginia; The Forest Primeval" by Conway Whittle Sams, 1916

TIMELINE: WHAT WAS GOING ON IN EUROPE	
1380	Wyclif supervises the English Bible translation.
1456	Gutenberg publishes the first printed Bible in Latin, in Mainz, Germany.
1492	Columbus makes first voyage to the Americas.
1509	King Henry VIII leads Parliament in breaking with the Catholic Church in 1534; becomes "supreme head of the Church of England."
1525	Tyndale's New Testament is published.
1547	King Edward VI advances Protestantism.
1553	Queen Mary Tudor, a Roman Catholic, comes to power in England.
1558	Queen Elizabeth I takes the throne and restores Anglicanism in England.
1603	King James VI of Scotland becomes King James I of Great Britain, continues the Anglican Church.
1625	King Charles I assumes power and marries Henrietta Maria, a Catholic, soon afterward.
1653	Oliver Cromwell, a Puritan, becomes "Lord Protector" of England, Scotland, and Ireland.
1660	King Charles II, a Catholic, is restored to the throne in Great Britain and commences the Restoration period.
1685	King James II, a Catholic, becomes king of England, Scotland, and Ireland.
1688	Queen Mary II & King William III, Protestants, come to power and reign Great Britain jointly.
1689	The Act of Toleration (Religious Freedom) is signed by Parliament in England.

PROTESTANTISM IN ENGLAND

King Henry VIII
(1491-1547)

Henry VIII

- King Henry VIII became King of England in 1509 and reigned until his death in 1547.
- He is best known for his six marriages.
- He initiated the English Reformation from papal authority over the annulment of his first marriage. He appointed himself the Supreme Head of the Church of England and dissolved convents and monasteries. He was excommunicated from the Catholic church.
- In 1534 King Henry VIII led Parliament in breaking with the Catholic Church.
- The Church of England became the official church of England with Henry as the head via the Act of Supremacy, making England a Protestant nation.

King James I

King James I

"The founding of Virginia was a movement undertaken by England for the extension of Protestantism...."

King James VI of Scotland became King James I of England in 1603. The land also included Scotland and Ireland, which led to the forming of Great Britain. He was a Presbyterian of strict upbringing.

On April 10, 1606, King James I signed "The First Charter of Virginia," which was drafted by Rev. Richard Hakluyt. Known as the "Defender of the Faith," King James I encouraged religious freedom all over Europe and sponsored the production of the English translation of the Bible for the Church of England in 1611.

Protestant Reformation

The Protestant Reformation was started as an attempt to reform the Catholic Church which had a complete domination all over Europe. It was protesting practices and doctrine in the Catholic Church. Martin Luther, and a group of fellow Catholic Monks, believed "the Word of God is perfect and pure; it is truth itself." The Bible alone was the source of the Christian faith, and not the Pope.

Martin Luther

Martin Luther
Wittenberg

1507 Monk Martin Luther was ordained in the Catholic Church and preached his first Mass. He became troubled about the spiritual conditions of the Catholic Church.

1517 Monk Martin Luther, at the age of 33, published 95 Theses on indulgences and nails the Theses on Wittenberg Castle Church doors in Wittenberg, Germany.

1519 Luther debates denied supreme authority of popes and councils.

1520 He was excommunicated from the Catholic Church for refusing to recant his publishing's. Luther believed "the understanding that God's righteousness is God's gift to us rather than the standard by which he judges us." Luther had strong support from his fellow monk friends and protection from territorial German princes. He theologically broke with the Church of Rome. He was forced to say that "popes and church councils could err and that the Bible alone could be trusted as an infallible source of Christian faith and teaching."

1525 Luther, a former monk, married Katharine von Bora, a former nun, on June 13, 1525, causing quite a reformation on marriage and family life. They lived together at his former cloister in Wittenberg, where they housed and taught students for the ministry. The former monastery was huge and provided ample space for students and many reform visitors.

1527 Luther wrote the hymn "A Mighty Fortress."

1534 Luther and his colleagues translated the Bible in German.

Founding of Lutherans

Martin Luther never considered founding a new denomination. He and his fellow monks just wanted to reform the Catholic Church. Moreover, to also reform the clergy from the selling of indulgences. "Indulgences were documents bought from the church either for themselves or on behalf of the dead to release either the purchaser or the deceased from purgatory for a certain number of years."

"Luther believed in and preached what he regarded as the historically reliable narrative of Jesus' life, death, and Resurrection in the four Gospels, a narrative anticipated in the Old Testament and further explained in the New. Christians are called to obey this Jesus and no other."

"Luther's teaching on the priesthood of all believers leveled the clergy to servants of the congregation—not enjoying a higher privilege than the laity, not even in their role as celebrants of baptism and the Lord's Supper."

Luther said, "The Word of God is perfect and pure; it is truth itself."

Reformation followers of Luther sprang up in Sweden, Norway, and Denmark. Word spread by the use of printing to reach a wider audience.

"Luther thought of the ruler as being supreme over the church in all such worldly matters as property and even organization, but he insisted that this authority stopped at the foot of the pulpit."

Renewal movement within Lutherans in the 17th century, and a revived Moravian Brethren movement centered in Saxony at Count Nikolaus von Zinzendorf's estate, had a huge influence on Europe.

Founding of the Church of England

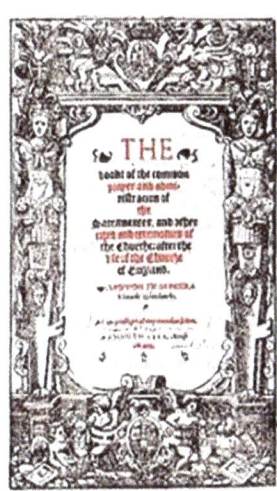

The Book of Common Prayer, 1549

In 1534 King Henry VIII led Parliament to break with the Roman Catholic Church and became the "supreme head of the Church of England." The first version of the Book of Common Prayer was published in 1549.

Mary Tudor became queen in 1553 and reestablished Roman Catholicism. Many Protestants were martyred, until Queen Elizabeth inherited the throne in 1558 and restored Anglicanism.

The Book of Common Prayer was required for public worship and the Archbishop of Canterbury was created to enforce uniformity in public worship.

The ruling king was ordained by God to govern their people as the king saw fit. His subjects had no rights. They might have had privileges granted by royal favor, otherwise they only had duties. Since the King of England was only accountable to God, he was the head of the Church of England and all his subjects must worship only in that church. This was known as the "Divine Right of Kings."

The Westminster Confession was drafted in 1646.

Founding of Puritans

Oliver Cromwell

Puritanism in England was a holiness movement, seeking holiness in the church, family, and community, as well as in personal life. It started around 1564. Certain clergy wanted more holiness in the Prayer Book.

Most Puritans were members of the established Church of England who wanted to reform the church from within. It was a movement to raise standards of Christian life in England. Like-minded people emerged. The Puritan era lasted from 1616 to 1691 in England.

Keeping Sabbath observance holy was how they got the name Puritan, "lived out in ministry, in discipline of daily life, in family, in secular vocations, and in the larger society."

They believed salvation, conversion, and reformation of the parish, and sang only psalms, no hymns.

When James I succeeded Elizabeth I in 1603, the Puritans had an influential minority in Parliament. James I and his son Charles I did not favor the Puritans. Many Puritans felt persecuted and left for Holland and America. Oliver Cromwell was elected to Parliament in 1628. He had great success as a military leader practicing religious freedom with his Puritan beliefs.

After defeating Charles II, the Scots and Irish, Cromwell set up a de facto leadership of Britain in 1653 as "Lord Protector" and dissolved Parliament. Cromwell was seen as a "Moses" figure. He established a Commonwealth form of Government. He also invited Jews to settle in England.

After his death in 1658 his son could not keep the government together, and Charles II came back as king. Puritan pastors were then ejected from parishes.

In 1689 Puritans regained freedom of worship through the Act of Toleration, along with other groups of worshippers.

Puritans were called "Nonconformists." "Pilgrims," were Puritan Separatists who fled to the Netherlands and then founded the colony at Plymouth, Massachusetts.

Founding of Quakers

George Fox, Quaker

In 1646 George Fox founded the Quaker movement in England.

Founder George Fox insisted that all people possessed an "inner light," which linked them to God and accorded them equal stature with each other.

Quakers were "taught self-denial, rigid abstinence from all luxury and self-indulgence." Quaker worship was to "wait on the Lord" and to "listen in silence to the still small voice inside each worshiper."

Quakers denied the absolute authority in the Bible. Instead they relied more on a "light within them." The rituals of baptism and communion, singing psalms in time of worship, the notion that places of worship are holy, and even strict observance of the Sabbath Day," were not observed.

The office of pastor was eliminated and women were encouraged to become leaders, though they did not believe wives should work.

Everyone led a very plain lifestyle. They would not serve in the military. Nor would they take an oath.

"The Presence in the Midst" by James Doyle Penrose

Reformers

John Calvin, Geneva

John Calvin (1509-1564) published the first edition of his *Institutes of the Christian Religion* in 1536. The City Council of Geneva commissioned Calvin in 1541 to reorganize the Church in Geneva, as it had declared for the Reformation years before, believing the Church must faithfully mirror the principles laid down in the Holy Scripture.

Calvin established a new organization with elders, deacons, and teachers to educate adults, children, and ministers. Later he established an Academy. He also established a fourfold ministry; worship, education, soundness and purity, and its works of love and mercy. "The principal work of the Spirit is faith… the principal exercise of faith is prayer." Prayer was key and what makes a Christian.

Calvin later believed in Predestination, the idea that "God does not indiscriminately adopt all into the hope of salvation but gives to some what he denies to others." "For all are not created in equal condition; rather eternal life is foreordained for some, eternal damnation for others."

The outworking of Predestination theology was a zeal for evangelism and wish for all to be saved. Geneva became a hub of a vast missionary enterprise. Sending missionaries to Italy, Germany, Scotland, and France, Calvin's homeland.

Community empowerment through burden sharing was how Calvin saw God's relation to his community.

Calvin was called "A Father of Democracy." To Calvin, "there was very clearly a Christian-biblical world-and life view which encompassed all phases of life—not just religion, but science, economics, and politics." "The church is not to rule the state." He also believed in "the principle of separation of the functions of church and state." The "church's form of government was to be fundamentally democratic" and "appointed by the people of the church as a whole."

Ulrich Zwingli

Swiss reformer, Ulrich Zwingli (1484-1531) 1519 in Zurich, Switzerland. Began the Swiss Reformation. By 1525 the reformation of the Church in Zurich was completed, by the use of force. "Zwingli allowed the civil ruler nearly total control over the church."

Jeanne d'Albret

French Huguenots. French Protestants led by Jeanne d'Albret who held to the Reformed or Calvinist traditions. Severe persecution under Louis XIV and Catholic hostility. Active in 16th and 17th centuries in France, about year 1560 when congregations first emerged. Forced to flee France due to religious and political persecution. Many settled in America.

John Knox

Scotch-Irish Reformers and Scots Reformers. Early part of the 16th century Martin Luther's teachings began to influence Scotland. John Knox spread Calvinism to Scotland. Knox had spent time in exile in Geneva and became a follower of Calvin. He set up settlements that adopted a Presbyterian system in Scotland, and rejected the most elaborate components of the Medieval Church.

Theodorus Frelinghuysen

Dutch Reformers. Started in the Netherlands around 1571, a severe believing group. Sent the first group to settle New Amsterdam in New York about 1628. Theodorus Frelinghuysen, a Dutch Reformer evangelist was sent to New York in 1720. In 1722 led a great revival starting in Germantown, PA., which spread to NY, NJ, and down the Shenandoah Valley in Virginia.

Count Nikolaus von Zinzendorf

Moravians Brethren. Renewed in 1722 by the Count at a Moravian settlement called Herrnhut, in Saxony, now in Germany, but then in Czechs. The Count renewed what Jan Hus, a Catholic priest, first started in the 15th century in Bohemia. Believed in "religion of the heart" and "faith and love over doctrine." Established a lifestyle of prayer, worship, a form of communal living, and a missionary movement. Strongly influenced John Wesley. Wesley visited the Count at Herrnhut, after experiencing first-hand the Moravian's calmness on his stormy voyage to America. Moravians later settled in Nazareth, PA and also in North Carolina.

Anabaptist Reformers. Started in Switzerland and Germany and linked with groups such as Amish, Mennonites, Hutterites, and Brethren. The movement began in 1525.

"Anabaptists would have nothing to do with the civil authorities. The responsibilities of the civil government, the Anabaptist said, were limited to non-Christians. True Christians did not require civil supervision, since they already obeyed God's law."

Founding of Presbyterians

John Knox

- John Knox (1505 - 1572) was a minister, writer, theologian, and leader of his country's Protestant Reformation in Scotland. He was ordained as a Catholic priest in 1532.
- Knox converted to Protestantism between 1543 and 1546. Defended George Wishart, a reformer that introduced Swiss Protestantism into Scotland. Wishart was arrested and murdered for his beliefs.
- Knox participated in a revolt at the castle of St. Andrews after Wishart's death, denouncing the Catholic Church. He hid at the castle and was captured by the French when they laid siege to the castle. He was later released.
- In 1549 Knox emerged in England as a paid preacher. In 1551 he became the chaplain to King Edward VI.
- Mary, Queen of Scots, came to the throne of England in 1553. Mary was Catholic. Knox's life was endangered.
- Knox left England, traveled to, and settled in Geneva.
- He became a believer of Calvinism. Called Calvin's Geneva, "the most perfect school of Christ that ever was on earth since the days of the apostles."
- Knox returned to Scotland for a visit in 1555 and organized Protestant congregations. He left under pressure and was burned in effigy in 1556. Back in England he led English congregations. He wrote many letters of encouragement back to Scotland.
- Knox arrived back in Edinburgh in 1559. He was pursued as a criminal but remained free.
- In 1560 he, along with Parliament, Knox formed a democratic form of church which was adopted with ministers and elders. Catholic worship was forbidden. Queen Mary, a Catholic, was driven from Scotland with Knox pursuing. Knox died in 1572 leaving an independent Scotland under a severe but democratically elected church.

- The Church of Scotland was founded in the 16th century by John Knox as an association of congregations. In 1560 it was adopted by Parliament in Scotland as the official Church, and in 1707 assured as the Scotland church created by the "Kingdom of Great Britain."
- Knox was predominately Calvinist, having studied under Calvin in Geneva while in exile.
- Predestination was one of the main doctrines.
- Followers became known as Presbyterians.
- Presbyterians were known to be well educated and wealthier than the common people.
- Presbyterians believed "Emphasis sovereignty of God, the authority of Scriptures, and the necessity of grace through faith in Christ."

Founding of Methodists

John Wesley

Charles Wesley

Around 1735, three out of four of all children baptized were dying under the age of five. Disease, workhouse curse of sin, and London was the center of England's distilling industry. One house in five sold spirits. Hangings were public attractions and morals were lost even in the established church. Clergy lacked morals, often took bribes, lacked spiritually, reverted to drunkenness, etc.

John Wesley and his brother Charles both were ordained in the Anglican Church, the established Church of England. Both brothers experienced spiritual awakening among the Moravians. Charles, while at Oxford University in 1729, founded the "Holy Club." They met "for prayer, devotional study, and religious conversation," and to seek God and break off destructive friendships. Also important to him was community outreach like teaching prisoners to read in jail. George Whitefield and John Wesley soon joined. A London paper assaulted the group in 1732, "this sect called Methodists." Fields rather than churches proved to be more productive sites for the work. Open-air preaching became the norm for evangelistic outreach and could far outnumber the seating capacity of the churches of the day.

Methodists believed in a personal relationship with Christ. They emphasized "sanctification as a gift of God's grace in a moment". And the importance of "growing in holiness through nurture and grace, and to spread scriptural holiness across the land."

Methodists rejected predestination.

John Wesley became the leader and soon organized his followers into small groups and strongly encouraged church discipline and small group accountability grounded in scriptural study and prayer. He also at the suggestion of his mother, supported lay preachers which was a "key distinctive of early Methodism: lay preaching."

Methodists were known as a singing people. Charles wrote hymns and John did the editing and printed hymnals.

"Wesley defended himself and his movement with the press, seeking both to dispel misunderstandings and to generate sympathy."

Wesley saw God's charge to the Methodist movement: "to reform the nation, particularly the Church; and to spread scriptural holiness over the land."

John Wesley Preaching On His Father's Tomb

Founding of Baptists

In 1609, the English General Baptist formed a small congregation in Amsterdam. In 1612 the small congregation moved to England in Spitalfields, outside London, during the reign of King James I. John Smyth was their minister. The congregation believed that "Christ died for all men" "not as Calvinists said, only for the elect."

Early seventeenth century Baptists in England emerged out of a Puritan-Separatist movement in the Church of England. It accepted only believers in Jesus Christ into its congregations, then baptized converts upon profession of faith. By 1625, several congregations mushroomed in

England. The Separatists were frustrated by the Puritans and wanted to separate from the Church of England.

Their opponents named them "Baptists."

Soon the Baptists led people to want more participation in their churches. By 1650 Baptists accepted total water baptism immersion for adult believers verses baby sprinkling. Defined as "plung'd over head and eares."

There were two groups, the General Baptists led by John Smyth, and the Particular Baptists under the influence of the teaching of John Calvin. The two groups later merged.

Baptist services were lengthy with Bible exposition, no singing, spontaneity and audience participation. By 1670 some churches were singing both Psalms and "man-made songs." The first Baptist hymnal was published in 1691.

The Baptists sought the faith of the New Testament church as first given by Jesus and his apostles.

Baptists struggled for religious freedom rather than one of toleration. In 1714 the General Assembly of Baptists in England commissioned Robert Norton to go to Virginia.

Timeline - Protestant Reformation

Protestant Reformation in Europe FOUNDED						
Church of England "Anglican"	Puritans	Quakers	Lutherans	Presbyterians "Reformers"	Methodists	Baptists
1534 King Henry VIII broke with Catholic Church	1564 Movement started in England	1646 England; George Fox	1517 Wittenberg, Germany; Martin Luther presents 95 Theses	1519 Swiss, Zurich; Ulrich Zwingli	1732 England; John Wesley, Charles Wesley, and George Whitefield	1609 First Church in Holland
1603 King James I, King of England; from Scotland; raised Presbyterian	1599 Oliver Cromwell; leader, Commonwealth government			1536 Geneva; John Calvin		1612 Moved to England during reign of King James I; first minister was John Smyth
1606 Virginia Charter; authored by Rev. Richard Hakluyt (Hachluit)	1641-60 Richard Baxter; Puritan leader / pastor; writer in Kidderminister			???? Scot-Irish; John Knox		
1611 King James I printed the Bible				1532 French Huguenots		1850 Adopted total water immersion for baptism
				1571 Dutch		
				1560 Presbyterians; John Knox		

PART II

Early America
Per 1606 Virginia Charter

*"Wee shall by plantinge (in America) inlarge the glory of the gospel…
and provide a safe and a sure place to receive people from all partes of the
worlds that are forced to flee for the truthe of Gods worde."*

ANGLICAN REV. RICHARD HAKLUYT, 1584

BACKGROUND

Before the settlement of Jamestown, on the island there was once an Indian village, Paspahegh, on the very spot. Also numerous-speaking tribes had lived thereabout. These tribes were part of the Powhatan Confederation.

The Spanish had also landed near Jamestown in 1525 on a spot on the James River shore which was apparently the same Jamestown peninsula. There Spain made its first unsuccessful attempt to settle the North America mainland. Led by Lucas Vasquez de Ayllon and authorized by King Carlos I of Spain, they settled on the peninsula which the English settlers later named Jamestown. De Ayllon died and his successors gave up and sailed back to Santo Domingo.

In 1570 a small unarmed Jesuit missionary expedition was sent to Christianize the Indians up the Chesapeake Bay. The Jesuits were aided by at first an Indian, Don Luis, whom they had brought with them as interpreter although he soon deserted them and joined the natives. Near the Chisakiack Indian village close to Queen's Creek on the York River, "they erected a log chapel and offered the first Mass in York County." The tomahawks of hostile Indians shed the first blood for Jesus Christ on the sod of Virginia," with the help of the treacherous Don Louis, leaving only one crazed young man to report to returning ships the next year", thus bringing an end to Spanish attempts at colonization above Florida.

Explorer Frenchman Verrazano (1524 – 1528) and Sir Walter Raleigh (1585 – 1586) were known to have explored the Chesapeake area. "If Verrazano may be called the discoverer of Virginia, Raleigh was her founder."

Colonization Attempts by England in America

England's effort to establish a colony in the new world, which began during the reign of Queen Elizabeth I, failed miserably. One settlement in Maine was abandoned because of the severe climate. Two others, on the Outer Banks of North Carolina, also were failures.

A fourth try, authorized by King James I after four storm-tossed months at sea, the three ships, the *Susan Constant*, *Godspeed*, and the *Discovery* arrived in Virginia.

King James I of England 1566 - 1625

King James I

Son of Mary, Queen of Scots, King James VI of Scotland became King James I of England in 1603, succeeding Queen Elizabeth upon her death. She had no children.

He was raised in a strict Presbyterian family and tutored with Calvin's theological influence. Scotland was part of the early Protestant Reformation led by John Knox, a Scot reformer, and a Calvin disciple.

First to be called king of Great Britain, he assumed the title in 1603. He ruled Scotland, Ireland, and England in what became called the Jacobean era.

He was very well educated, a writer and author. He signed "The Charter of Virginia, April 10, 1606."

THE FIRST CHARTER OF VIRGINIA

Anglican Rev. Richard Hachluit (also spelled Hakluyt)

Author and Visionary of the "The First Charter of Virginia
April 10, 1606"

"He did more than any man of his generation to invigorate the efforts which eventually bore fruit in Virginia and New England."

"Richard Hakluyt is known today as the "Father of Colonization."

Reverend Richard Hachluit

- Born in 1552 and died in 1616 at the age of 64.
- Orphaned at age of five, his father had dedicated him to the Lord as a baby.
- The Queen provided for his education at Westminster, and after his father's guild sent him to Oxford.
- He studied, taught, and lectured at Christ Church from 1570 to 1583.
- Around 1575 God called him to be a pastor.
- He fell in love with a well-to-do lady, but she did not want to marry a pastor. He chose to follow God's calling on his life.
- God gave him a vision for the colonization of America.
- He carried this vision for over 30 years to take the gospel to the New World (America). His vision shelved until after Queen Elizabeth's death.
- This vision was based on Psalm 107: 23&24; "others went out on the sea in ships: they were merchants on the mighty waters. They saw the works of the Lord, His wonderful deed in the deep."
- Hachluit was the author and visionary of "The First Charter of Virginia, April 10, 1606."
- He was a man of the cloth – "Clerk, Prebendary of Westminster."
- The Virginia Company was a business venture to carry the gospel of Jesus.
- His cousin, Mr. Richard Hakluyt (older), a lawyer, was a prayer intercessor in the court of King James I.

- Hakluyt documented John Cabot's voyages, as well as Sir Gilbert voyages to the New World. He also documented Sir Gilbert's half brother, Sir Walter Raleigh's, attempted settlement at Roanoke Island.
- In 1583, he was appointed chaplain to the English embassy in Paris, France.
- Hakluyt was buried in Westminster Abbey.
- Today Hakluyt Society (travel) in Great Britain is named after him.

The First Charter of Virginia, April 10, 1606

JAMES, by the Grace of God, King of England, Scotland, France and Ireland, Defender of the Faith, &c. WHEREAS our loving and well-disposed Subjects, Sir Thorn as Gales, and Sir George Somers, Knights, **Richard Hackluit, Clerk, Prebendary of Westminster**, *and Edward-Maria Wingfield, Thomas Hanharm and Ralegh Gilbert, Esqrs. William Parker, and George Popham, Gentlemen, and divers others of our loving Subjects, have been humble Suitors unto us, that We would vouchsafe unto them our Licence, to make Habitation, Plantation, and to deduce* **a colony of sundry of our People into that part of America commonly called VIRGINIA**, *and other parts and Territories in America, either appertaining unto us, or which are not now actually possessed by any Christian Prince or People, situate, lying, and being all along the Sea Coasts, between four and thirty Degrees of Northerly Latitude from the Equinoctial Line, and five and forty Degrees of the same Latitude, and in the main Land between the same four and thirty and five and forty Degrees, and the Islands "hereunto adjacent, or within one hundred Miles of the Coast thereof;*

And to that End, and for the more speedy Accomplishment of their said intended Plantation and Habitation there, are desirous to divide themselves into two several Colonies and Companies; the one consisting of certain Knights, Gentlemen, Merchants, and other Adventurers, of our City of London and elsewhere, which are, and from time to time shall be, joined unto them, which do desire to begin their Plantation and Habitation in some fit and convenient Place, between four and thirty and one and forty Degrees of the said Latitude, alongst the Coasts of Virginia, and the Coasts of America aforesaid: And the other consisting of sundry Knights, Gentlemen, Merchants, and other Adventurers, of our Cities of Bristol and Exeter, and of our Town of Plimouth, and of other Places, which do join themselves unto that Colony, which do desire to begin their Plantation and Habitation in some fit and convenient Place, between eight and thirty Degrees and five and forty Degrees of the said Latitude, all alongst the said Coasts of Virginia and America, as that Coast lyeth:

We, greatly commending, and graciously accepting of, their Desires for the Furtherance of so noble a Work, which may, by the **Providence of Almighty God, hereafter tend to the Glory of his Divine Majesty, in propagating of Christian Religion to such People, as yet live in Darkness and miserable Ignorance of the true Knowledge and Worship of God, and may in time bring the Infidels and Savages, living in those parts, to human Civility, and to a settled and quiet Government:** *DO, by these our Letters Patents, graciously accept of, and agree to, their humble and well-intended Desires;*

And do therefore, for Us, our Heirs, and Successors, GRANT and agree, that the said Sir Thomas Gates, Sir George Somers, **Richard Hackluit**, *and Edward-Maria Wingfield, Adventurers of and for* *our City of London, and all such others, as are, or shall be, joined unto them of that Colony, shall be called the first Colony; And they shall and may begin their said first Plantation and Habitation, at any Place upon the said-Coast of Virginia or America, where they shall think fit and convenient, between the said four and thirty and one and forty Degrees of the said Latitude; And that they shall have all the Lands, Woods, Soil, Grounds, Havens, Ports, Rivers, Mines, Minerals, Marshes, Waters, Fishings, Commodities, and Hereditaments, whatsoever, from the said first Seat of their Plantation and Habitation by the Space of fifty Miles of English Statute Measure, all along the said Coast of Virginia and America, towards the West and Southwest, as the Coast lyeth, with all the Islands within one hundred Miles directly over against the same Sea Coast; And also all the Lands, Soil, Grounds, Havens, Ports, Rivers, Mines, Minerals, Woods, Waters, Marshes, Fishings, Commoditites, and Hereditaments, whatsoever, from the said Place of their first Plantation and Habitation for the space of fifty like English Miles, all alongst the said Coasts of Virginia and America, towards the East and Northeast, or towards the North, as the Coast lyeth, together with all the Islands within one hundred Miles, directly over against the said Sea Coast, And also all the Lands, Woods, Soil, Grounds, Havens, Ports, Rivers, Mines, Minerals, Marshes, Waters, Fishings, Commodities, and Hereditaments, whatsoever, from the same fifty Miles every way on the Sea Coast, directly into the main Land by the Space of one hundred like English Miles; And shall and may inhabit and remain there; and shall and may also build and fortify within any the same, for their better Safeguard and Defense, according to their best Discretion, and the Discretion of the Council of that Colony; And that no other of our Subjects shall be permitted, or suffered, to plant or inhabit behind, or on the Backside of them, towards the main Land, without the Express License or Consent of the Council of that Colony, thereunto in Writing; first had and obtained.*

And we do likewise, for Us, Our Heirs, and Successors, by these Presents, GRANT and agree, that the said Thomas Hanham, and Ralegh Gilbert, William Parker, and George Popham, and all others of the Town of Plimouth in the County of Devon, or elsewhere which are, or shall be, joined unto them of that Colony, shall be called the second Colony; And that they shall and may begin their said Plantation and Seat of their first Abode and Habitation, at any Place upon the said Coast of Virginia and America, where they shall think fit and convenient, between eight and thirty Degrees of the said Latitude, and five and forty Degrees of the same Latitude; And that they shall have all the Lands, Soils, Grounds, Havens, Ports, Rivers, Mines, Minerals, Woods, Marshes, Waters, Fishings, Commodities, and Hereditaments, whatsoever, from the first Seat of their Plantation and Habitation by the Space of fifty like English Miles, as is aforesaid, all alongst the said Coasts of Virginia and al raerica towards the West and Southwest, or towards the South, as the Coast lyeth, and all the Islands within one hundred Miles, directly over against the said Sea Coast; And also all the Lands, Soils, Grounds, Havens, Ports, Rivers, Mines, Minerals, Woods, Marshes, Waters, Fishings, Commodities, and Hereditaments, whatsoever, from the said Place of their first Plantation and Habitation for the Space of fifty like Miles, all alongst the said Coast of Virginia and America, towards the least and Northeast, or towards the North, as the Coast lyeth, and all the Islands also within one hundred Miles directly over against the same Sea Coast; And also all the Lands, Soils,

Grounds, Havens, Ports, Rivers, Woods, Mines, Minerals, Marshes, Waters, Fishings, Commodities, and Hereditaments, whatsoever, from the same fifty Miles every way on the Sea Coast, directly into the main Land, by the Space of one hundred like English Miles; And shall and may inhabit and remain there; and shall and may also build and fortify within any the same for their better Safeguard, according to their best Discretion, and the Discretion of the Council of that Colony; And that none of our Subjects shall be permitted, or suffered, to plant or inhabit behind, or on the back of them, towards the main Land, without express Licence of the Council of that Colony, in Writing thereunto first had and obtained.

Provided always, and our Will and Pleasure herein is, that the Plantation and Habitation of such of the said Colonies, as shall last plant themselves, as aforesaid, shall not be made within one;hundred like English Miles of the other of them, that first began to make their Plantation, as aforesaid.

And we do also ordain, establish, and agree, for Us, our Heirs, and Successors, that each of the said Colonies shall have a Council, which shall govern and order all Matters-and Causes, which shall arise, grow, or happen, to or within the same several Colonies, according to such Laws, Ordinances, and Instructions, as shall be, in that behalf, given and signed with Our Hand or Sign Manual, and pass under the Privy Seal of our Realm of England; Each of which Councils shall consist of thirteen Persons, to be ordained, made, and removed, from time to time, according as shall be directed and comprised in the same instructions; And shall have a several Seal, for all Matters that shall pass or concern the same several Councils; Each of which Seals, shall have the King's Arms engraver on the one Side thereof, and his Portraiture on the other; And that the Seal for the Council of the said first Colony shall have engraver round about, on the one Side, these Words; Sigillum Regis Magne Britanniae, Franciae, & Hiberniae; on the other Side this Inscription round about; Pro Concilio primae Coloniae Virginiae. And the Seal for the Council of the said second Colony shall also have engraven, round about the one Side thereof, the aforesaid Words; Sigillum Regis Magne Britanniae, Franciae, & Hiberniae; and on the other Side; Pro Concilio primae Coloniae Virginiae:...

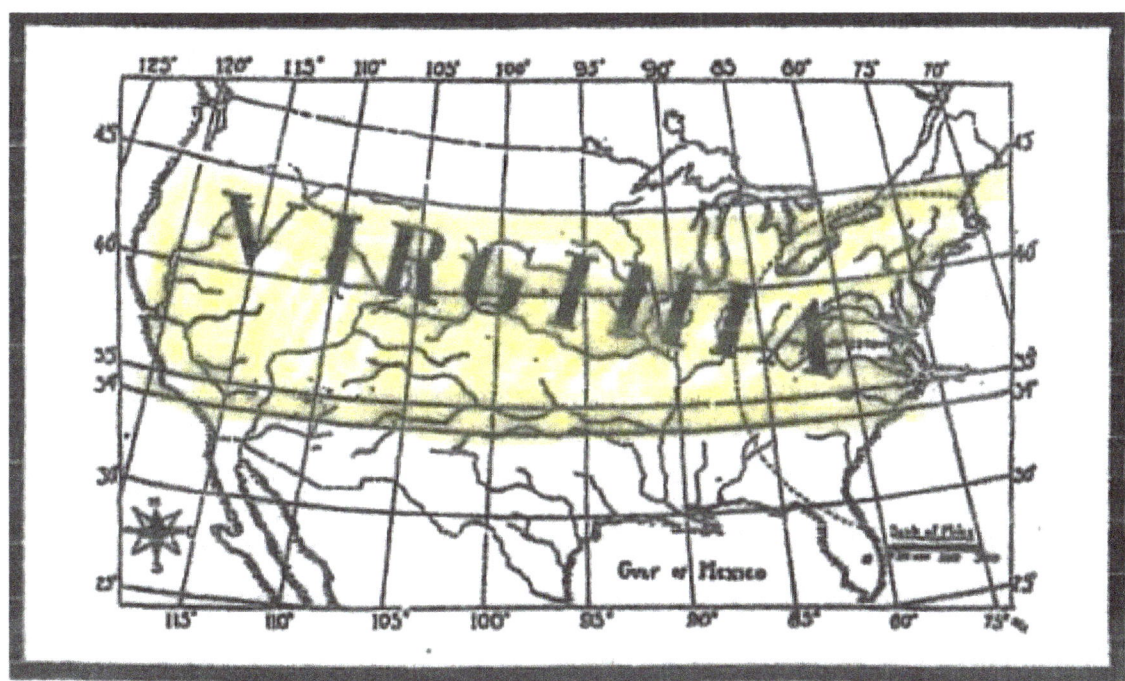

Map of Virginia at the Time of the First Charter of Virginia, April 10, 1606

The First Charter of Virginia was authored by Anglican Rev. Richard Hachluit (Hakluyt), and represented the author's original vision for the colonization of the New World. Based on Psalm 107:23-24, Rev Hakluyt envisioned the 1606 Virginia Company Charter to be a business venture that would carry the gospel of Jesus to America. *"Others went out on the sea in ships; they were merchants on the mighty waters. They saw the works of the Lord, his wonderful deed in the deep." Psalm 107:23-24*

Hakluyt had studied navigation, voyages, and travel from a small child under the direction of his cousin, a lawyer and geographer. He put together the most comprehensive collection of maps and information on the land called Virginia.

Hakluyt was a prolific writer. "Readers of Hakluyt's "Voyages" satisfied their curiosity aroused by the talk they heard in public houses of new discoveries and travels to distant places….Proof of the Anglican minister's importance to this movement was his membership among the applicants for a charter for the Virginia Company. More than any other person he had prepared the public mind for action on Western planting."

The Discourse Concerning Westerne Planting was an eloquent plea for English settlements in America for these objects: (written by Hakluyt in 1583 and presented to Queen Elizabeth I):
- To extend the Reformed Religion.
- To replace other English trades which, thanks to Spain, have grown "beggarly or dangerous."
- To supply England's wants from her own dominions, instead of from foreign countries.
- To employ "numbers of idle men."

- To provide overseas bases in the event of a war with Spain.
- To enlarge the Queen's revenues, and increase the Royal Navy.
- And, finally, that hardly perennial, to discover that Northwest Passage.

Hakluyt also foresaw America as a land where persecuted Christians could find refuge. "Wee shall by plantinge (in America) inlarge the glory of the gospel…and provide a safe and a sure place to receive people from all partes of the worlds that are forced to flee for the truthe of Gods worde." – Rev. Richard Hakluyt, 1584

Purpose

The purpose of the 1606 Charter was "so noble a Work, which may, by Providence of Almighty God, hereafter ten to the Glory of his Divine Majesty, in propagating of Christian Religion to such People, as yet in Darkness and miserable Ignorance of the true Knowledge and Worship of God, and may in time bring Infidels and Savages, living in those Parts, to human Civility, and to settle and quiet Government:…"

Land Area

King James I of England originally granted a charter in 1606 to the Virginia Company which defined two colonies in an area from Bermuda to the West Coast, to today's South Carolina all the way to Maine and parts of Canada. The area, which now encompasses almost all of America, was called Virginia.

Territory one was the London Company – between 34 degree and 41 degrees latitude (Jamestown)

Territory two was the Plymouth Company – between 38 degrees and 45 degrees latitude (Plymouth) (the overlap was for whoever got here first)

THE FIRST CHARTER OF VIRGINIA | 29

1606 - 1621

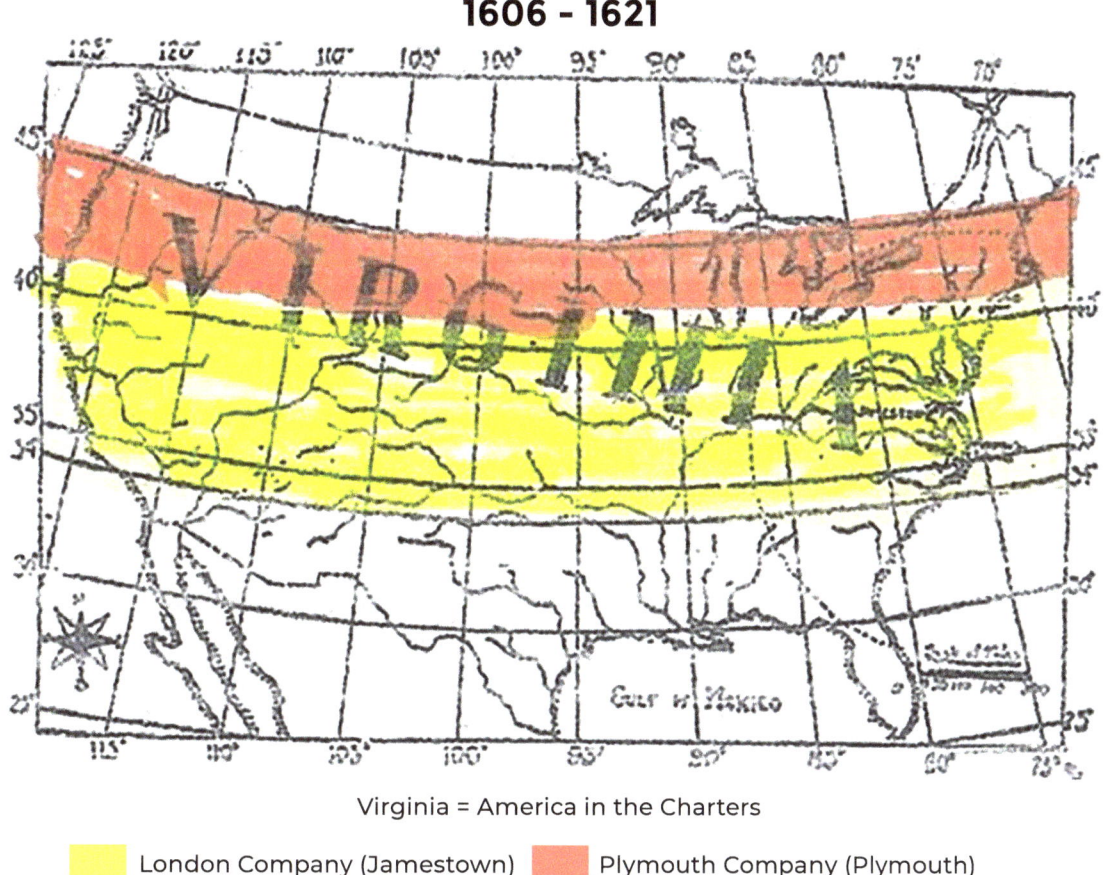

Virginia = America in the Charters

London Company (Jamestown)   Plymouth Company (Plymouth)

FIRST NATION PEOPLE, NATIVE AMERICANS

What They Believed
By Chief G. Anne Richardson, Chief of the Rappahannock Tribe, Virginia

Who is the Holy Spirit? He is one of the Trinity, the third man of the Godhead. The Father, the Son and the Holy Spirit. For purposes of understanding what I am about to write, I will attempt to identify for you who these supernatural beings are in the Native American culture. Native Americans have always understood and had a close relationship with the Creator or as we know Him today, God the Father. They were well acquainted with the interactions of the Great Spirit in their ceremonies, dreams, visions, fasts and morning prayers or as we know Him today as, the Holy Spirit. Native people have always believed in and interacted with the spirit realm seeking supernatural intervention and guidance. They understood the power and authority of the Creator God and they feared Him.

Guardians of the Land

I believe that Indigenous people have an innate spiritual knowledge gifted them by the Creator when He gave them their inheritance, as the first- born sons of this land. As the inheritor, Native people were held responsible for and given authority to care for and be watchful stewards over the inheritance He had given them. This is validated by the examples we see set both in the Bible and in Jewish practice. The inheritance is given to the first-born son. Therefore, these spiritual truths and authority over the land is woven into their traditional culture and they live by it and walk it out in their daily lives. Although colonial powers usurped the physical possession of the land, their spiritual authority and care for the land is still very alive and well all these generations later. However, because their religious beliefs were so ancient, I don't believe they had knowledge of Jesus the Christ, because He did not exist when their traditional beliefs were passed down to them.

Chief Anne Richardson

When European powers came to the New World, the established religions rejected the Native traditional beliefs and ceremonies as pagan and it was all outlawed.

Europeans saw the power inherent in Native ceremonies and feared them because they couldn't control the supernatural. Then the colonials began to force Native people to worship and believe as they did. Some Natives rejected this new religion but most embraced it to please the colonists and keep the peace for their people. The English used the word; "civilized" to politically subdue the Natives through this new religion equating it to a more organized, structured worship that could be controlled. I think of all the atrocities that have been done to the Native Americans by foreign powers, to date this is by far the greatest destruction that could ever have been done. Now they had to cut their hair, put on English clothes, forsake their ceremonies, dreams and visions and the interactions they had with the spirit realm, to set inside of a wooden building, in a quiet and controlled box. The sweet liberty and freedom they had known to interact with the spiritual world had been taken away. As in every group, there is always someone who practices the opposite, but primarily their creation stories, a belief in an all-powerful, supreme god, beliefs in good and evil were all present in their traditional religious structure. There were stories passed down of supernatural visitors who taught them how to care for and respect the land and each other. The Natives believed that all of creation was sacred and they applied that principle in their everyday lives. Having studied the Bible for years, I have concluded that Native people received instruction from God in many different ways, just as He does with us today. He visits us where we are and gives us what we need, no matter who we are or where we come from. What a mighty God we serve!

My Tribe had early interactions with several European religions and each tried incessantly to change who we were. We had to basically become English in order to be considered a Christian. Even in my early years of seeking the Lord, attending church outside my community and trying to fit in with some denominations, I was still perceived as a Pagan. It was a stronghold of the mind that was passed down generation, to generation from the colonial period. God help us to overcome the lies the enemy has used to divide God's people both racially and denominationally!

Virginia Algonquian Population Estimates, 17th Century

	1608	1608	1610/1611	1669	1703	First / Last mentioned
	Smith 1612 (339-341)	Smith 1624 (347-348)	Strachey 1953 43-46, 64-69)	Haning 1809 - 1823,2: 274-275)	Beverley 1705 (232-233)	
POWHATAN GROUP						
Appamatuck I	200	200	400	165	30	1607/1705
Arrohateck	100	100	200	-	-	1607/1611
Cantauncack	-	-	335	-	-	1608/1629
Caposepock	-	-	1,335	-	-	1608/1611
Cattachiptico	-	-	1,000	-	-	1608/1611
Chesapeake	335	335	335	-	-	1585/1627
Kecoughtan	65	65	100	-	-	1607/1610
Kiskiack	135-165	135-165	165	50	-	1607/1677
Mattaponi	100	100	465	65	-	1607/present
Menapacunt	-	-	335	-	-	1608/1611
Nansemond	665	665	665	150	100	1585/present
Orapaks	-	-	165	-	-	1608/1611
Pamareke	-	-	1,335	-	-	1608/1611
Pamunkey	1,000	1,000	1,000	165	135	1607/present
Paraconosko	-	-	35	-	-	1608/1611
Paspahegh	135	135	135	-	-	1607/1610
Potaunk	-	-	335	-	-	1608/1611
Payankatank	135	135	135 - 165	-	-	1608/1611
Potvhayick	-	-	-	100	-	1661/1669
Powhatan	135	135	165	35	-	1607/1670
Quacohamaock	-	-	135	-	-	1608/1611
Quiyoughcohannock	85	85	200	-	-	1607/1627
Shamapent	-	-	335	-	-	1608/1611
Warraskoyack	135	135	200	-	-	1585/1627
Weanock	335	335	500	50	almost wasted	1607/1707
Werowocomoco	135	135	135	-	-	1607/1611
Youghtanund	200	200	235	-	-	1607/1611
Chichahominy	665	835	1,000	200	55	1607/present
Appamatuck II	-	-	-	35	-	1608/1669
Cuttatawomen I	100	100	100	-	-	1608/1656
Cuttatawomen II	65	65	65	-	-	1608/1611
Matchotic I	335	335	335	-	-	1608/1659
Matchotic II	-	-	-	-	-	1652/1669
Moratico	265	265	265	135	-	1608/1669
Nansatico	500	500	500	165	-	1608/1705
Opiscopank	-	-	-	-	-	1608/1611
Pissasec	-	-	-	-	-	1608/1611
Potomac	535	665	535	-	-	1608/1666
Potopaco	-	-	-	200	17	1669/1703
Rappahannock	335	335	335	100	a few families	1608/present
Secacawoni	100	100	100	-	-	1608/1660
Tauxenent	135	135	135	-	-	1608/1675?
Wicocomoco	435	435	435	235	10	1608/1719
Total	9,365 - 9,395	9,695 - 9,760	14,185 - 14,215	1,850	347+	

The Principal Portion Of The Territory Ruled By Powhatan

Chief Powhatan, the Indian leader of a confederacy of Algonquian speaking Virginia Tribes, after hearing a prophecy from his priests to be aware of men coming from the East, "Sunrise," "from the Chesapeake Bay," took this to mean his enemies the Chesapeakes. Accordingly, he completely obliterated that tribe.

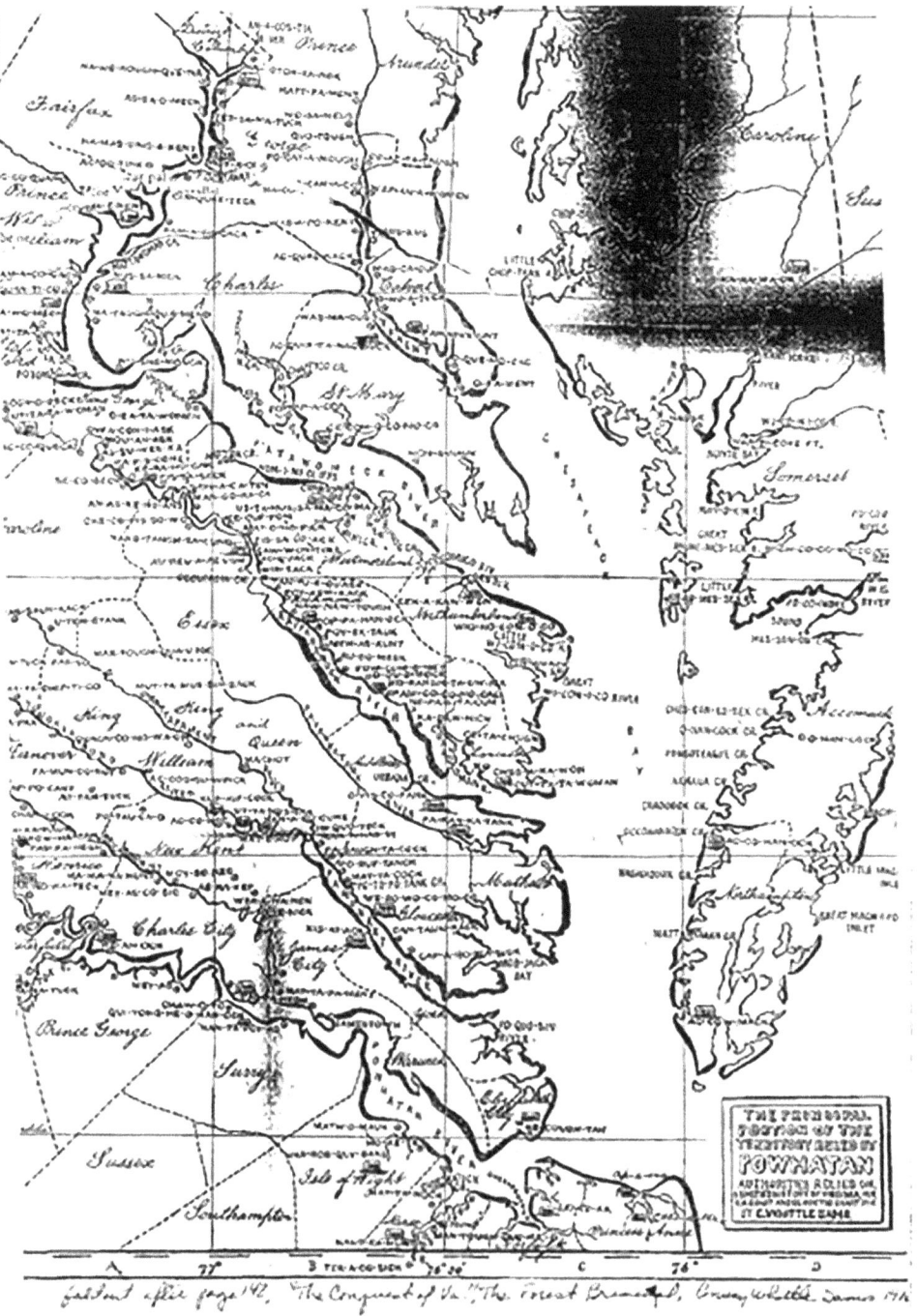

PART III

Establishment of Protestant Churches in Virginia

"We are one body, we have one Name, one Gospel, one Christ, one God, one Holy Spirit, one heaven."

Reverend Francis Asbury, 1803

ESTABLISHMENT OF PROTESTANT CHURCHES IN VIRGINIA

1606 Charter under Church of England

The 1606 Charter stated that the Church of England was to be the Church of Virginia. Christian religion was to be "preached, planted, and used" both within the plantations and among the savages "according to the doctrine, rights, and religion now professed and established within our realme of England."

The Charter's guarantee in the fifteenth paragraph that the colonists should enjoy the rights of Englishmen was simply declaratory of the principle that the colonists who settled on the territory claimed by England and who recognized their allegiance to the English crown were to enjoy the liberties of "the Realm of England or any other of our said dominions."

The Charter was not proposing a new nation, but an extension of England.

London Company First to come to Virginia (Jamestown 1607)

The London Company arrived first in 1607, and the Plymouth Company arrived second in 1620.

1606 - 1621

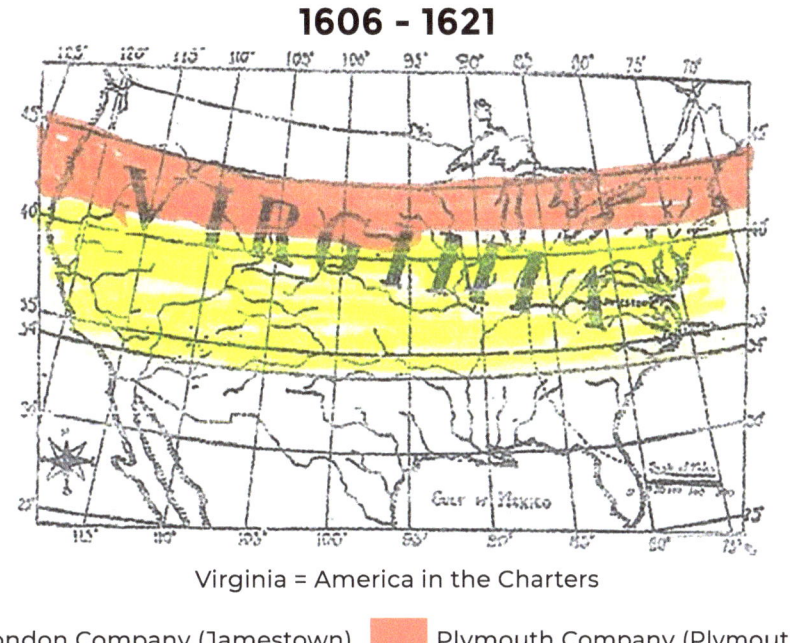

Virginia = America in the Charters

London Company (Jamestown)   Plymouth Company (Plymouth)

Planting the Cross at Cape Henry

The Landing at Cape Henry, April 1607

Cape Henry is a point of land at the mouth and entrance to the Chesapeake Bay. This site was the first landing in the new world for the settlers (105) and crew (40) of the group of the Virginia Company that would become the first English permanent settlement at Jamestown in 1607. After four storm-tossed months at sea, the three ships, *Susan Constant*, *Godspeed*, and the *Discovery* arrived April 26, 1607.

Rev. Robert Hunt, because of the strife aboard, called for three days of prayer and fasting. The company came ashore April 29, 1607, and named the place Cape Henry for the King's son, Henry, Prince of Wales. The settlers planted a wooden cross and claimed the land for God and King. They had a time of thanksgiving, prayer, and worship.

Anglican Rev. Robert Hunt Prayer
1568 -1608

Reverend Hunt
First Protestant
Minister

Rev. Robert Hunt, the spiritual leader for the expedition, spoke the words, **"from these very shores the Gospel shall go forth to not only this New World but the entire world."**

This was a covenant made in response to the vision and purpose of the New World colonization, a prophecy of things to come for the Virginia area.

Virginia Early History by Date

April 10, 1606	Virginia Company Charter founding Jamestown & Plymouth (Visionary: Rev. Richard Hakluyt - Psm. 107:23-24
December 20, 1606	Settlers (105) and Seamen (40) set sail from England
April 26, 1607 (or May 6th)	Cape Henry Landing - first group go ashore. (three days prayer and fasting called by Rev Hunt.)
April 29, 1607 (or May 9th)	Cape Henry named and cross erected by Reverend Robert Hunt and company "from these very shores the Gospel shall go forth and no not only this New World but the entire world"
April 30, 1607	Stop at "Old Point Comfort" explore James River area
May 13, 1607	Arrive at Jamestown
May 14, 1607	Disembark at Jamestown
July 6, 1610	Nansemond Indians kill one settler
July 9, 1610	Gov Gates takes revenge and wipes out Kecoughtan Indians at "Old Point Comfort"
September 1611	Citie of Henricus founded (now part of Richmond)
April 13, 1613	Pocahontas brought to Jamestown as prisoner and hostage
April 5, 1614	Pocahontas baptised and married John Rolfe
March 1614	Tabacco shipped to England by Rolfe
1614	Four principle settlements: Jamestown, Kecoughtan, Henrico, Charles City
May 1616	Rolfe's sailed for England
July 30-August 4, 1619	First Virginia General Assembly (met in church at Jamestown Island)
1619	First Africans in volume arrive in America. Entered as indentured servants not slaves.
July 31, 1619	Henricus Colledge founded, America's first college
March 22, 1622	Indian Massacre butchered 347 men, women, & children. Jamestown saved by Pamunkey servant Chanco

1622-1630	White mens revenge against Openchancanough
1625-1632	York River settled
1632	Williamsburg first settled
1634	Colony divided into eight counties (shires)
1653	Oldest Indian reservation on Pamunkey River
1661	Virginia Monarchests codified slavery
September 19, 1676	Bacon's rebels set whole town of Jamestown in flames
May 29, 1677	Middle Plantation Treaty with Indians
1698	State House at Jamestown burned
1699	Capital moved to Williamsburg

Jamestown Early History by Date

1614	**Four Principle Settlements**		
	Jamestown	Kecoughan	Henrico
	Charles		
1634	**Colony Divided into Eight Shires**		
	Original Name	*changed to*	*Current City/County*
	Accawmack		Northamton County
	Charles City		Charles City County
	Charles River		York County
	Elizabeth City	Kecoughton	City of Hampton
	Henrico		Henrico County City of Richmond
	James City		James City County
	Warrosquyoake		Isle of Wight County
	Warwick River		City of Newport News
1636	New Norfolk	Part of Elizabeth City	
1637	Isle of Wight County	changed from Warrosquyoake	Isle of Wight County
	Lower Norfolk	Park of New Norfolk	City of Norfolk
			City of Virginia Beach
			City of Portsmouth
			City of Chesapeake
	Upper Norfolk	Park of New Norfolk (along Nansemond River) and into North Carolina	
1642	Nansemond	Upper Norfolk renamed	City of Suffolk plus (1974)
1646	Nansemond County		Extending into parts of Isle of Wight County and Southampton County

Virginia Settlements and Colonies

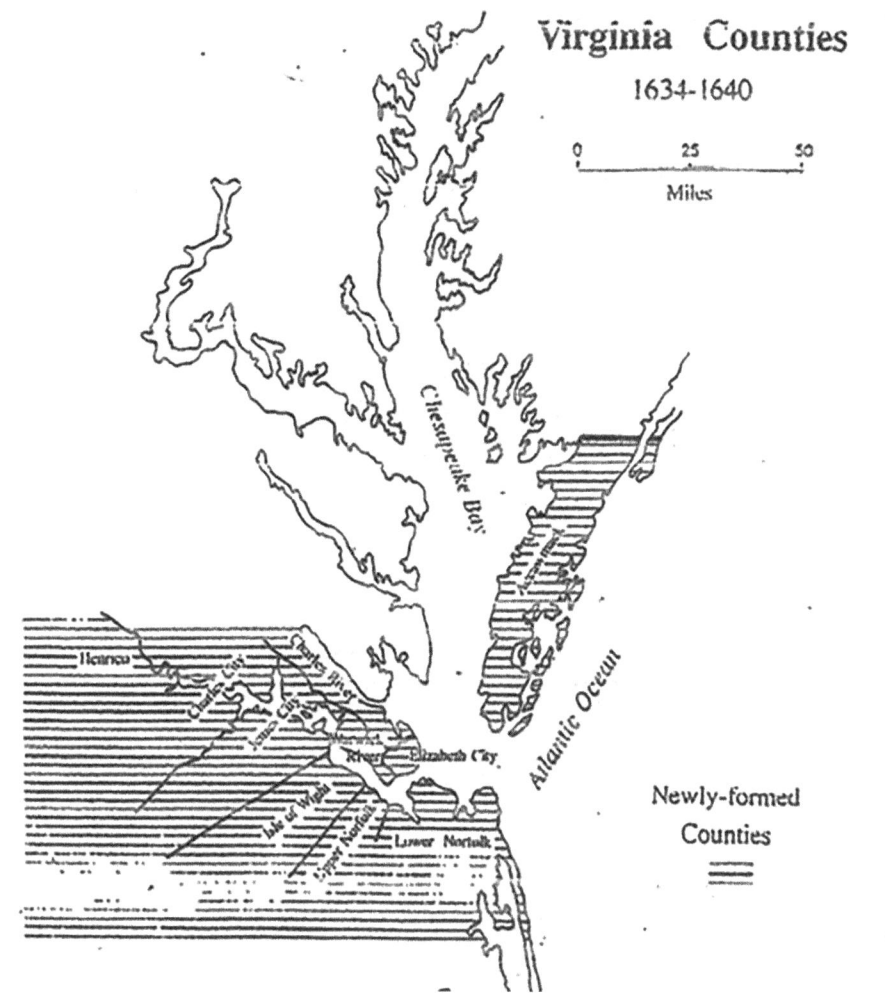

Map of Virginia Counties

Timeline - Early Protestant Denominations Churches in Virginia

Early Protestants in America						
Church of England "Anglican"	**Puritans**	**Quakers**	**Lutherans**	**Presbyterians "Reformers"**	**Methodists**	**Baptists**
1607 Rev. Robert Hunt planted cross at Cape Henry, VA	1620 Pilgrims; Plymouth, MA; John Winthrop; William Bradford 1660 Movement died out	1655 South of the James River; Elizabeth Harris 1672 Nansemond County; George Fox	1703 Falckner swamp; NY, DE, PA 1749 Philadelphia, PA area	1625 Dutch New Amsterdam 1718 William Tennet; evangelist, son, and brother 1720 Dutch T. Frelinghuyser; revivalist; NY, NJ, PA, VA 1734 New England; Jonathan Edwards 1776 John Witherspoon; minister, signer of Declaration of Independence	1736 Savannah, GA; John and Charles Wesley 1738 Savannah, GA; George Whitefield 1771 Philadelphia, PA; Francis Asbury	1638 First Church in Providence, RI; Roger Williams 1682 Church in Kettery, ME; moved to SC; first in South 1707 Congregations in PA, NJ 1750 First African American Church in SC 1760 Brown University started

Early Protestants in Virginia						
Church of England "Anglican"	**Puritans**	**Quakers**	**Lutherans**	**Presbyterians "Reformers"**	**Methodists**	**Baptists**
1607 Jamestown; Rev. Robert Hunt 1619 Virginia General Assembly; parishes established 1763 Dinwiddie County; Rev. Devereux Jarratt, revivalist	1628 Nansemond County; Richard Bennett 16?? IOW County; Edward Bennett, was persecuted and left VA for MD	1655 South of James River for 5 years; Elizabeth Harris 1672 Nansemond County; George Fox	1714 Madison County; German Iron Workers 1717 Madison County; Indentured Servants to Gov. Spotswood 1720s Down Shenandoah Valley, VA; German / Dutch Reformers; included Lutherans, Mennonites, Brethren, and Monrovians	1687 Eastern Shore; Francis Makemie (ended upon his death) 1700 Manakintown, VA on James River; Huguenots 1740 Samuel Morris; "Morris Reading House" 1748 Hanover County; Samuel Davis	1772 Norfolk, Portsmouth, Suffolk; Robert Williams 1772 Joseph Pilmoor; first Methodist Society in VA 1775 Francis Asbury	1714 Southside of James River; Robert Norden 1727 Burleigh (Burewells Bay) 1774 Renamed Mill Swamp Baptist 1759 Western Branch 1787 John Leland

CHURCH OF ENGLAND

First Protestant Church Service

According to John Smith, "For a Church we did hang an awning (which is an old sail) to three or foure trees to shadow us from the sunne. Our walls were rales of wood. Our seats unhewed trees, till we cut planks, our Pulpit a bar of wood nailed to two neighboring trees."

"It was here that the founder of the first Protestant church of America, Rev. Robert Hunt, preached twice each Sunday, read the morning and Evening prayers, and celebrated communion once every three months. A special prayer was composed for the colonists that was repeated each morning:

Almighty God,... we beseech Thee to bless us and this plantation which we and our nation have begun in Thy fear and for Thy glory… and seeing Lord, the highest end of our plantation here is to set up the standard and display the banner of Jesus Christ, even here,….Lord let our labour be blessed in laboring for conversion…. Lord sanctity our spirits and give us holy hearts, that so we may be Thy instruments in this most glorious work."

"First Church Service" by Scottie Marshall

"It was spring, when the travelers arrived, and the spring reminds me of the new beginnings that were happening to each of these men. I put one of the ships in the background on the right side, to show that it didn't have it's sails, but the empty masts left the shape of crosses. I had tried to put the preacher, Robert Hunt, between the two neighboring trees as he would sharing God's Word... but erased him... which kind of makes him look like a distant memory in our history, but very important and to not be forgotten.... The Bible, God's Word, is still living, and still a critical part of history. I put the three eagles to represent, The Father, the Son, and The Holy Spirit, Who had watched over these men and the ships, as they journeyed across the Atlantic Ocean, filling the sails with His Wind, (and we still need the Wind of the Holy Spirit to blow across the land in this country in these days). I didn't realize I had put a cross beside the altar...His wind, is what filled those ship's sails, that carried them along the course that He had prepared for them." - Scottie Marshall

First Convert

Pocahontas was baptized in 1614 as the first known convert. She was baptized in the church at Jamestown. She was the daughter of the Indian Chief Powhatan who had saved the life of John Smith. She also helped secure peace between the Indians and settlers as well as obtain needed food. John Smith said that she was "next under God… the instrument to preserve this colony from death, famine, and utter confusion."

Picture from US Capitol Rotunda, Baptism of Pocahontas

First Marriage

The Wedding of Pocahontas with John Rolfe, lithograph by Geo Spohni, c. 1867

Pocahontas married John Rolfe in 1614. Chief Powhatan consented to the marriage and sent an uncle to represent him at the wedding.

First Thanksgiving

"First Thanksgiving" by Sidney King

Four men, William Throckmorton, Richard Berkeley, George Thorpe, and John Smyth formed the Berkeley Company out of London England. They commissioned Dr. John Woodlief, a surgeon from Bristol, to lead the expedition on September 4, 1619. Woodlief had been to the New World several times and survived the "Starving Time" at Jamestown in 1609 and 1610.

Woodlief commissioned the "Good Ship Margaret", 35 feet long, to carry hand-picked settlers. They came as indentured servants to claim 8,000 acres on the King James River, with 3 miles waterfront, for farming, building homes, etc. They were indentured for 3 to 8 years, and each given 15 to 30 acres.

They left Bristol, England on September 16, 1619, and after sailing in very close living quarters, a stormy voyage, and a very stressful sailing, they arrived in the New World. On December 4, 1619, at Berkeley Hundred later called Berkeley Plantation, settlers numbering 38, came ashore 24 miles southwest of Richmond, Virginia on the King James River. They came ashore led by Captain John Woodlief, and kneeling gave thanks for the safe passage.

The first Thanksgiving "was all about prayer not food." Under orders of the Berkeley Company their arrival was to "be yearly and perpetually kept holy as a day of Thanksgiving to Almighty God." Thus the First Thanksgiving in the new world, America. The day was to be a solemn affair focused on prayer; it was not a festival of food as in Massachusetts.

Berkeley Plantation was one of the first plantations in America. It is in Charles City, Virginia. In 1619 Benjamin Harrison III purchased the land, and his son later built a three story mansion on the property.

First Representative Government Convened

First Virginia Assembly, Sydney King

The Virginia General Assembly was first convened at Jamestown in the church, on July 30, 1619, and continues today in Richmond. It is the third oldest continuous legislature in the world, ranking behind Iceland, which began in 930, and Great Britain's dating from 1265. The Virginia Assembly was a model for the U.S. Congress.

James Fort

"James Fort" built in May and June, 1607, Sydney King

The Church of England (Anglicans) brought the formal gospel of Jesus Christ into the colonies, coming first to Virginia. God chose the Anglicans, their message, their organizational abilities, their funds, their people, and their willingness to colonize the New World. The colony was preserved with total support of England's crown and people.

Maps of Early Anglican Parishes

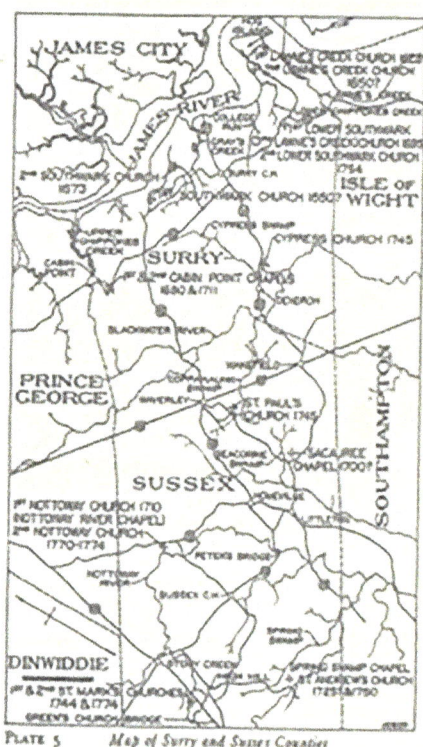

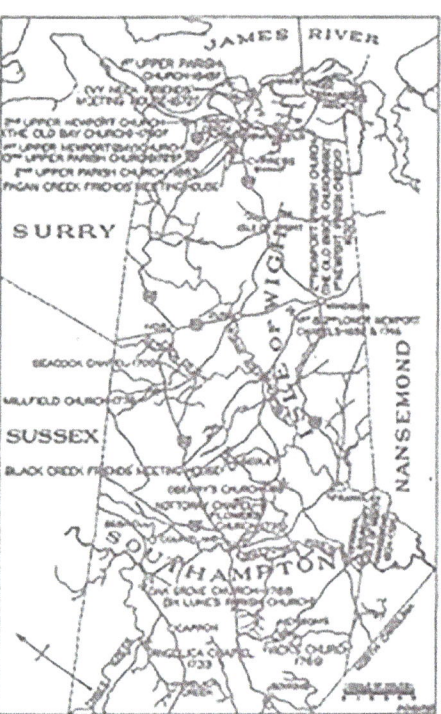

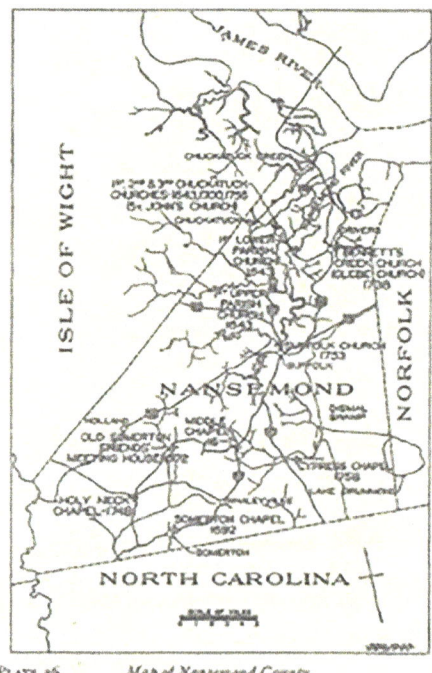

More maps can be found in "Colonial Churches of Tidewater Virginia" by George Carrington Mason, 1945

The Virginia Colony was an outpost of Protestantism. There was a distinct difference between the Virginia Settlement and the Massachusetts Settlement.
- The Virginia Settlement at Jamestown "was in harmony with, and an extension of, the national aims and aspirations with the" Church of England with "no grievance against the mother country." It represented the whole of England and the King. Per the King's instructions they were to be ruled by a Council not a single man.
- The Plymouth Settlement in Massachusetts only represented "a fraction of the English nation. Puritanism was obnoxious to the English Government." After leaving England for Holland and staying only one year, they moved back to England for ten years in peace and security. Then they looked elsewhere to separate themselves from England. When the Pilgrims arrived thirteen years later, a representative government had already been established, and Protestantism planted at Jamestown.

PURITANS, "INDEPENDENTS"

Early Puritans

Brave In A New World: After three months at sea, the first American Puritans, the Pilgrims, landed in December 1620, Governor William Bradford wrote, "The had now no friends to welcome them nor inns to entertain or refresh their weatherbeaten bodies, no houses or much less town to repair to. ... And for the season, it was winter. ... What could they see but a hideous and desolate wilderness? ... What could now sustain them but the Spirit of God and his grace?"

- From 1547 to 1558, this group wanted reformation and change within the Church of England, believing man was only governed by God, not state, nor king.
- 1558 Elizabeth became Queen of England. She was deeply attached to the reformation when she began her reign. She had a problem assuming the title of the head of the church. Elizabeth brought Protestantism back into favor again.
- Around 1564, Puritan congregations began in England. Each group was self-organizing and independent, varying in standards and admission to church membership, baptism and serving of communion. They were seeking holiness, advancing the Kingdom of God,

and Christian families. "The Puritans were people on a mission: to create a pure church and a thoroughly Christian society."
- Puritans in England were in touch with other protestant reformers in Scotland (Knox), France (Huguenots), Swiss (Calvin), Germans (Lutherans), and Dutch. They had conferences concerning common causes and beliefs. I.e. Zurich in 1553.
- Queen Elizabeth died in 1602. In her later years of her reign she persecuted the Puritans.
- James VI, King of Scotland, became James I King of England in 1603. Born in Scotland, he was brought up in a strict sect, protestant, Presbyterian home. He died at 59 years old in 1625.
- King James I signed the 1606 Charter to colonize the new World as written by Rev Richard Haackylt. The charter was a business venture to preach the gospel. The London Company made it first to Virginia in 1607, and the Plymouth Company arrived in 1620 at Cape Cod, Massachusetts.
- King James I printed the King James Bible in 1611.
- Puritans were still persecuted. James Robinson of Leyden, England had a congregation of about 300 souls. A group left for Amsterdam in 1608 because of the persecution, but came back to England.
- 1620 James Robinson's congregation organized some members to go to the New World. Robinson stayed behind to lead the rest of the congregation.
- The two Ships, *Mayflower* and *Speedwell* left August 2, 1620. Repairs had to be made on the *Mayflower*, and discouraged colonists on the *Speedwell* returned. Finally, September 6, 1620 100 souls, men, wives, and infants, sailed. It was a 63 day voyage that landed on December 1620 in Plymouth.
- William Bradford (1588-1657) was the leader of the segment of the congregation migrating to America.
- The "Mayflower Compact" dated Nov 11, 1620, pledged the group, "solemnly and mutually in the presence of God and one another," to "covenant, and combine together into civil body politic." The good of the colony, not the interests of any individual, was to be the guiding principle.
- Lawyer John Winthrop (1588 – 1649) was the second Governor and leader of the group.
- The Puritan colonists regarded themselves as loyal subjects of England.
- The "Pilgrims" were the radical, and strict group of the Puritans.
- The creation of the Massachusetts Bay Company, "Bay Company," in 1629, replaced the Plymouth Company of 1606. The charter was granted by Charles I.
- A decade after their arrival in 1620, the Pilgrims were almost the sole European settlers in New England. In 1630 another 700 sailed with John Winthrop in March and another 300 arrived shortly afterwards, and another 1000 that same year.
- In 1631 John Eliot emigrated to America to evangelize the Indians. He learned the Algonquian language, and in 1663 published the entire Algonquian Bible, the first Bible

printed in America. Eliot organized Indian towns of "praying Indians", and trained some natives as ministers.
- 1637 brought the Pequot War. Colonists mounted war, burning 600 Indians, men, women, and children. An Indian nation disappeared, it brought out the worst point in the puritan character. When their passions once inflamed their religion, itself was cruelty.
- In 1638, the first Black from the West Indies, for an exchange for Indian captives taken in the Pequot War of 1637.
- By 1640, Puritans could claim four colonies in New England: Massachusetts, Connecticut, Rhode Island, and New Haven.
- The Puritans solemnly observed the Sabbath. Professing a mission of gospel holiness, they fulfilled it but in part. When opposed they were revengeful and cruel.
- Clergyman Roger Williams in 1635 was banished from a New England Massachusetts colony and started a new group in Providence, Rhode Island. Rhode Island became a sanctuary for dissenters and other groups such as Baptists. In 1643, Williams got his own charter from England for Rhode Island. Williams took refuge with the Narragansett Indians, and he bought land from them for a new colony.
- Business and wealth started overtaking the society as not all new arrivals had the same puritan views.
- Oliver Cromwell, a Puritan, in 1649 became the Puritan Commonwealth leadership until 1658.
- From 1630 to about 1660, Puritan control of New England was virtually complete. Church, state, and society followed guidelines established by the Puritan founding fathers. This was a result of a new wave of immigrants less committed, as New England became an economic opportunity. The Puritan exiles entered a career of wealth, and independence, and earthly fame.
- One of the often-stated purposes of Puritan colonization was the conversion of the Indians. In 1646 they made four visits to Waaubon's. Success. They wanted to learn to pray in their own language, and offered their children to be educated.
- When Charles II returned to the throne in 1660, the 12 year reign of Puritan values was forced to end in England. So did the American hope of a permanent English reformation.
- After 1660 the Puritan homogeneity of New England began to disintegrate.
- 1675 brought disastrous Indian uprisings.
- After King James I came Charles I, who was no friend of the Puritans. He married a Catholic from Spain. She governed England with her values.
- The education of their children was based on reading of the Bible. The other mainstay was The New England Primer.
- Puritans started Harvard College in 1636 in Cambridge, Massachusetts, designed for the training of ministers.
- The colonial settlement in New England, as envisioned by its founders, was a failure.

- By 1730, New England bore little resemblance to the biblical commonwealth envisioned by Winthrop and others. Even the Great Awakening of the 1730s and 1740s could not revive the Puritan spiritual fever.

Puritans in Virginia
Richard Bennett of Early Nansemond County, Virginia

- Richard Bennett (? – 1674) was born into a wealthy, influential, English merchant family.
- Richard's uncle, Edward Bennett, was an auditor of the Virginia Company in London in 1621. He was patented a large property in what is now Isle of Wight. Edward had grants of land on the James River, Nansemond River, and Maryland.
- Richard Bennett, a Puritan, settled around the James River in Nansemond County.
- Bennett brought into Nansemond County the first Africans as indentured servants.
- In 1629 he served as a Burgess, and in 1631 as the Commissioner of the district.
- He became a member of the Governor's Council in 1642.
- In the 1630's Richard Bennett was granted 2000 acres on the Nansemond River in Virginia for having imported 40 persons, as well as land near Craney Island. He transported over 600 settlers from England to the colony.
- His land was called "Welcome Plantation," and "Bennett's Choice."
- He was one of the first Independents, Puritans, in Nansemond County.
- Bennett was one of 3 Major Generals in the Colonial Militia.
- He was, and is, called the "First Citizen of Nansemond County."
- In 1642, Richard Bennett sent his brother Philip to Boston petitioning for three Puritan ministers. They came and only stayed for a few months because newly appointed Gov. Berkley ordered that non-conformists to the Church of England depart the colony. Berkley nailed many churches shut.
- Puritans like Richard Bennett settled in the 1620's in Upper Norfolk County (now Nansemond County), his brothers Phillip and Robert in Nansemond County, and his uncle Edward in Isle of Wight County. Richard was given land grants in 1635, 1637, 1638, etc, along the eastern side of the Nansemond River (2500 acres) and Craney Island.
- In 1649, Richard Bennett and other Puritans (77 families) left Nansemond County because of persecution by Gov. Berkeley. They moved to Maryland and founded Annapolis. Another 60 families left and settled on the Patuxent River in Maryland. They abandoned their farms and everything. Bennett was the leader of the South-of-James River Dissenters (Puritans).
- Bennett and others moved back to Virginia in 1652, when Oliver Cromwell, a Puritan who established a commonwealth form of government in England, named Richard Bennett Governor of Virginia.

- That same year Cromwell sent a fleet of armed ships and 900 soldiers to Virginia to oust Gov. Berkeley.
- Richard Bennett in 1652 to 1655 was Virginia's first Governor of the Commonwealth, at the request of Oliver Cromwell, a Puritan. Cromwell disposed of Charles I as King of England in 1649. Cromwell died in 1658.
- Between 1655 and 1657, Bennett met Elizabeth Harris, a Quaker, at his plantation. She "convinced" him.
- In 1656, Bennett was an Agent for Virginia in England.
- Bennett was again a member of the Governor's Council in 1658.
- In 1660, Berkeley again became Governor after Cromwell died and Charles II came back from exile.
- By 1664, after the "Act for Suppressing Quakers", only two little Quaker groups remained in Virginia; *Chuckatuck* with Thomas Jordan and his wife Margaret; the group met in their home and others came by boat. Jordan and wife were both imprisoned. They suffered much but kept on meeting. Sheriff carted away their possessions. And *Nassawaddox* on the Eastern Shore. These two groups were the two to hold out successfully for the right to worship God their way.
- In 1672, George Fox, founder of the Quakers in England, was welcomed by Richard Bennett in Nansemond County. Bennett returned to live in Maryland.
- In 1674, Bennett willed part of his plantation (300 acres) to "Glebe" Bennett Creek Chapel, for the benefit of the Parish poor. He willed 2000 pounds of tobacco to four of the Nansemond Quaker neighbors. Two Quakers were also executors of Bennett's will.
- His daughter Anne was also a Quaker
- Bennett died in Maryland in 1674 a Quaker.
- "The Richard Bennett Trust," established to benefit the poor, is the oldest trust in America and still exists.

QUAKERS

Early Quakers "Friends"

- George Fox Started the Quakers in England in 1646.
- Quakers were enthusiasts and revolutionaries with passion for words. Sharing there is 'something of God in you. Turn your mind within…examine your heart…try your ways, with the Light Christ Jesus had enlightened you.'
- Men and women could speak out as non-conformist to the Church. By 1655, there were about 20,000 Quakers in England
- By 1642, there were almost as many Puritans as Royalists in England.

George Fox

- Bennett came back in 1652 when Oliver Cromwell named him governor. Oliver Cromwell sent a fleet of armed ships and nine hundred solders to support Bennett taking back the governor's position from Berkley. Bennett was governor until 1655.
- In 1655, Quakers appeared in Virginia first with Elizabeth Harris visiting the south of the James River area for almost five years. She preached out-of-doors.
- Harris spoke to the dissenting remnant, Puritans, in Norfolk, Nansemond, and Isle of Wight Counties. Governor Berkeley had harassed these southside people over their failure to support the established church. She convinced former governor Richard Bennett, a Puritan of Nansemond County, who had returned from Maryland and was the leader of the south-of-James River Dissenters. Harris then went up to Maryland to visit the dissenters who left Virginia in 1649.
- Bennett's land was near the mouth of the Nansemond River and the James River. The plantation was called "Welcome Plantation," "Bennett's Choice."
- Quakers were called "Children of the Light".
- Quakers were persecuted by local authorities by order of Governor Berkeley in 1642.
- They had striven to end war, and stood for peace, and against violence, change the penal system and aided Native Americans.

- By the time Berkeley arrived in Virginia in 1642, there were quite a few Quaker in three meeting places: Elizabeth River Church in Lower Norfolk County (now Norfolk and Portsmouth), East, and Chuckatuck in Nansemond County.
- In 1659, Berkeley was again governor. As he had rooted out the Puritans in 1640, he now set out in 1660 to evict the new non-conformists, the Quakers.
- "Quaker movement is based on the conviction that there is some thing of God in every human being. The Friends call this divine thing 'the inward light' or 'the light of Christ". The Quakers worship is to "wait on the Lord;" that is to listen in silence to the small voice inside each worshiper.
- In the first 50 years of the Quakers' existence, the Friends great word was TRUTH. In the 1750s they emphasized LOVE when describing the nature of God and the spirit of Christ, integrity and incomparable human sympathy.
- The Quakers described slavery as evil.
- They lost interest in attracting new members, and began to reach out to serve unfortunates. Attending the plight of black people was a first step.
- Quakers were vocal, disruptive, and against civil authority, ie. refusing to doff hats in church and court.
- In 1672, George Fox, founder of the Quakers in England, visited Nansemond County and was welcomed by Richard Bennett.
- Also in 1672, the Quaker Meeting House in Chuckatuck and Somerton was established. Chuckatuck was defined as the entire peninsula between the Nansemond River and Chuckatuck Creek. Other meeting places south of the James included Terrascoe Neck (near Brewers Creek), Pagan Creek, Western Branch, Southern Branch.
- At the First Continental Congress in 1774, 6 delegates were Quakers out of 55. They called for a boycott of British goods.
- In 1775, it was determined that "All Quakers ….. shall be exempted from serving in the military."
- Quaker fanaticism could be violent.
- Six little meetings south of the James were Chuckatuck, Terrascoe Neck, Pagen Creek, Western Branch, Southern Branch and Somerton, around 1684.
- An area south of the James River was called "Quaker Neck" peninsula between Bennett's Creek and now Western Branch.
- Quakers were quite active in forming our American founding issues, documents, and congress.

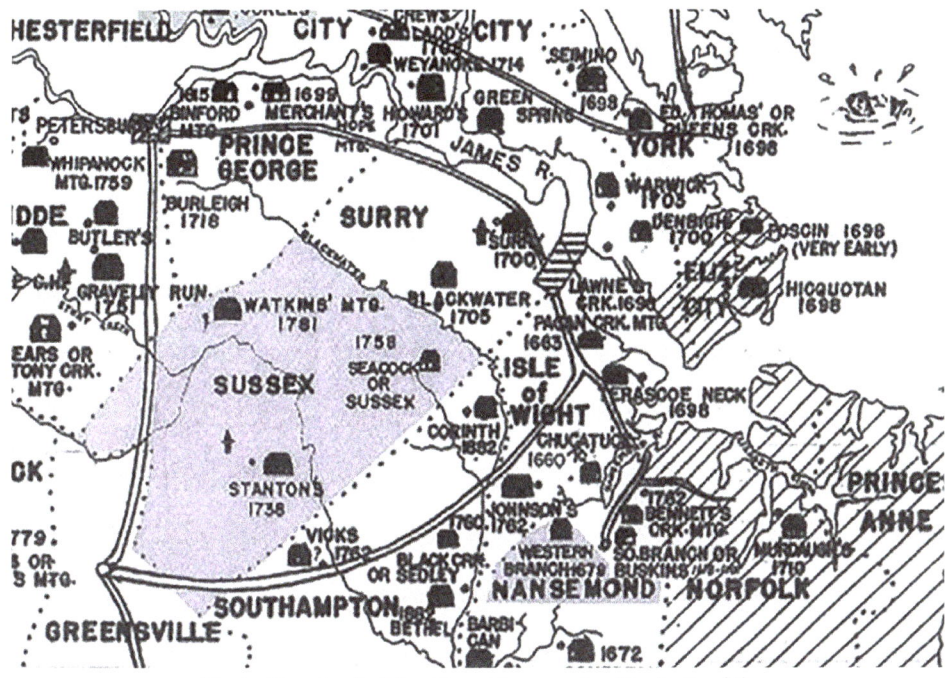
Early Quaker's Meeting Houses by Karla Smith

LUTHERANS

- Founded by Martin Luther in Wittenberg, Germany in 1514.
- Luther only wanted to reform the Catholic Church, and the Pope excommunicated him.
- His message was justification by faith.
- In exile he translated the Bible into German.
- Alexander Spotswood became Governor of Virginia in 1710 until 1722. He was interested in trade with the Indians and mining. Indians were mining gold, silver and copper in designated creeks and rivers.
- In 1714, twelve German Reformer families (42 people) from Nassau-Siegen Forest, moved along the Rapidan River in Virginia, at a place called Germanna. They were indentured servants for 7 years to Governor Spotswood of Virginia, working in their expertise of Ironworks. They had moved from Germany to England, then to Virginia.
- "First German Reformed Church on continent" doubled as a defensive blockhouse.
- In 1714 Gov. Spotswood also established Fort Christanna in Brunswick, Virginia. This later became the center for Lutherans, Methodists, and Baptists
- In 1716, a mining operation was started at the silver mine.
- In 1717, a second group of German Reformers/Lutheran immigrants, 20 families of 80 people, arrived in Virginia. The group had planned to go to PA. They settled at "Germanna Track." The Hebron Lutheran Church was established in Madison County. It remains the oldest continuing Lutheran church in the country.
- In 1720, additional German Reformers/Lutheran groups immigrated to Virginia (40 families) and settled along the Licking Run.
- They were led by reverend John Henry Haeger (1644 - 1737).
- 1722 brought a revival among the German Reformers in Germantown, PA. This was the beginning of the Great Awakening among the German/Dutch Reformers in 1726 ingathering, that came to the Shenandoah Valley.
- In 1740, Hebron Lutheran Church was built in Madison County with funds from Germany. It is the oldest continuous Lutheran Church in American.

Early Lutherans

- In 1748, Henry Muhlenberg in Penna established the first Lutheran Body in America.
- By 1820, Lutherans settled up the Shenandoah Valley mostly from Augusta County throughout Rockingham, Page, Shenandoah, Frederick, and Clarke Counties in Virginia.
- A lack of trained ministers from Germany accounts for slow growth.

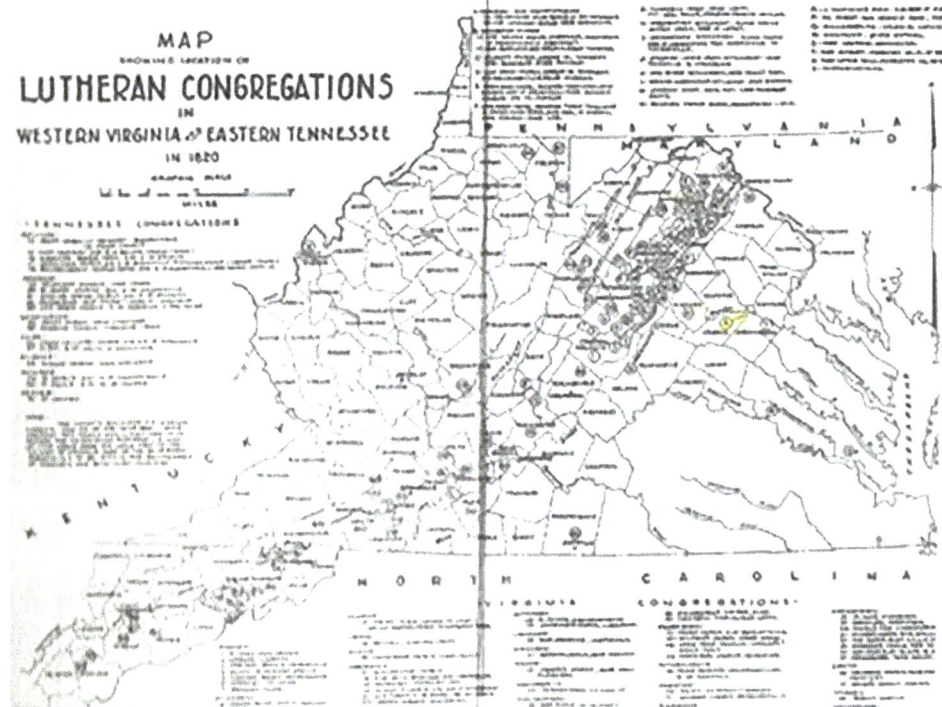

EARLY PRESBYTERIANS IN VIRGINIA (REFORMERS)

- In 1683, Francis Makemie came to Masosin near Richmond.
- Makemie did Church planting in the Eastern Shore, Accomack County Virginia, starting in 1687.
- Francis Makemie had served several congregations on the Eastern Shore in Accomax County. First coming in 1687, he was considered as the pioneer of the Presbyterian denomination.
- Makemie died in 1708. Not one church survived after his death. No new Presbyterian churches were planted for 30 years until the Scotch-Irish arrived.
- Reformers (Presbyterians) in Virginia:
    - Dutch Reform: Settled in New York as New Amsterdam, and New Jersey. From Netherlands
    - Geneva Reform: John Calvin originated. Jonathan Edwards, Rev John Witherspoon.
    - Swiss Reform: Ulrich Zwingli, Zurich 1510
    - French Reform, Huguenots: 1700 at Manakintown and Sabot in Goochland County on the James River.
    - Scotch Reform: Francis Makemie 1687 Eastern Shore. Prime in USA. John Knox.
    - Swedish Reform: Amish, Mennonites, Brethren.
- Hanover County, Virginia, was the center of the Great Awakening in the South, "the cradle of Presbyterians" in eastern Virginia. Belief in predestination became the first dissenting movement which seriously impaired the supremacy of the Established Church.
- Rev. William Robinson was the first Presbyterian minister to preach in Hanover County. This was in 1742-1743.
- Rev. Robinson was an evangelist, who also held prayer meetings, and introduced singing of Psalms in their worship.
- Already in progress was an awakening attributed to Samuel Morris, a bricklayer. He had printed a copy from the Williamsburg Gazette of George Whitefield's sermon in Williamsburg Dec 16, 1739. The sermon was "What think ye of Christ?" He shared this

Francis Makemie

sermon plus more in first his home. The name "Morris's Reading House" was given to a meeting house he built because his home became too small. Soon, "Morris was invited to travel long distances in order to read to congregations."

- "The Reading House could not contain all that came, so meetings were held out of doors."
- Next came Samuel Davis who accepted the pastoral charge in Hanover and surrounding counties in 1748. With John Blair as a revivalist, "One night in particular a whole house full of people was quite overcome with power of the word, particularly of one pungent sentence and they could hardly sit or stand or keep their passions under proper restraint." Davis was the "earliest hymn writer of Colonial Presbytery."

Samuel Davis

- George Whitefield came and spent four or five days rekindling and revitalizing the earlier awaking in the Hanover area in October of 1745.
- Huguenots (French) settled in 1700 at Manakintown and Sabot in Goochland County on the James River.
- Hampton Sydney College was the first Presbyterian "Log College" in the South.

BAPTISTS

Early Baptists in Virginia

- In 1714, the General Assembly of Baptists in England commissioned Robert Norden as a "Messenger" to America. He applied in Prince George County Court for a license. He made his home in Prince George County along with his wife.
- That same year saw the initial Baptist planting in America, on the south side of the James River, Prince George County, Surry County, and Isle of Wight County in Virginia.
- In 1699, Baptists were mentioned in York City, now Yorktown, meeting at a Quaker Meeting house. Both groups, Baptists and Quakers, were dissenters and recipients of tolerance. There was a "cordial relationship that existed between Baptists and Quakers."
- The Canterbury Baptist Church in Kent County, England sent funds for "propagating the gospel" in Virginia in 1713/14.
- The Baptists had a three-fold order of ministers: Messengers, Elders, and Deacons. "Messengers were officers of the denomination, whereas the Elders and Deacons were officers of the local congregation."
- Robert Norden, as a Messenger, devoted himself to cultivating the Baptist faith by traveling over the area to teach, and conduct meetings with small groups in homes. He made his home in Prince George County, an area that included Surry, Isle of Wight and neighboring communities. He died in 1725.
- In 1727, the first society was formed in Burley (Burleigh) (Burewells Bay) in Isle of Wight. Richard Jones was the first ordained Elder. Later, in 1774, the society was constituted as Mill Swamp Church with elders David Barrow and Edward Mintz.
- Mill Swamp Church was called the "Mother Church," as it established churches at Smithfield, Moore's Swamp, Tucker Swamp, and Bethesda.
- "With the Baptists the struggle becomes one for religious freedom rather than one for toleration."
- "Baptists presented the great evangelical movement in the way which appealed most strongly to the masses; and their preachers, who generally lacked the heavy classical education of the day, possibly for this reason, addressed the ignorant with more effect."
- Daniel Marshall made a declaration of faith under the preaching of Whitefield. He settled at Sandy Creek in Guilford County, North Carolina. He expanded his ministry of

evangelism to other parts of southside Virginia. Sandy Creek became a part of the Great Awakening in Virginia.

- In 1776, the Baptist part of the Virginia Convention at Williamsburg, supported "separation of church and state," the Bill of Rights, and the end of Anglican established taxes.
- In 1778, John Leland settled in Orange County and became a leader of the Virginia Baptists. He was a contemporary of James Madison and Thomas Jefferson.
- In 1779, at Western Branch at Shoulders Hill Road, Nansemond County, Mission of Mill Swamp, Elders Barrow and Mintz "were dragged to the Nansemond River dipped until nearly drowned…order to depart and never return." They did return and a church was established.

The Dunking of David Barrow and Edward Mintz

- The Virginia government provided a foundation for America's founding documents. Madison and Jefferson worked first in Virginia and then for America. For example,
  - Declaration of Independence
  - The Virginia Bill of Rights
  - A Bill for the Establishment of Religious Freedom
  - The Constitution of the U.S. Freedom
  - First ten Amendments to the Constitution
- The Baptists were very involved with the development of all of these documents.
- From 1827 to 1831, the Mill Swamp Baptist revival was led by Rev. Daniel, resulting in a "great outpouring of the Spirit of God, one hundred and fifty were added to the church in about four months."
- In 1858, the Mill Swamp revival with Rev. John Ward added "nearly two hundred and fifty to the church."
- Baptists suffered a variety of persecutions in Virginia, ie. beatings, mob attacks, plunged into rivers, live snakes and hornet attacks, jailed, exposed to dangerous fumes, accused of being false prophets, fined for non-attendance at Church.
- The Baptist revival in 1755 started in Guilford County, NC, and spread to Sandy Creek Baptist church in Sandy Creek, NC, under the leadership of evangelist Daniel Marshall. Marshall "believed in direct leadership of the Holy Spirit." The power of God.
- The Baptist revival then moved up the current Route 29 to Orange and Culpepper Counties in 1759. The whole valley was affected by the revival.
- Also in 1785 to 1789, Baptist revivals occurred in Virginia, the Northern Neck (between the James River and Potomac River), King and Queen County, Carolina, Culpepper, Orange, Madison, Spotsylvania, Louisa, and Fairfax.
- The "Baptists carried to conclusion the attainment of religious liberty."
- Baptists became the dominant denomination in Virginia, appealing to black and white, rich and poor, and the masses.
- "Their preachers who generally lacked the heavy classical education of the day, possibly for this reason, addressed the ignorant with more effect." They appealed to the masses.

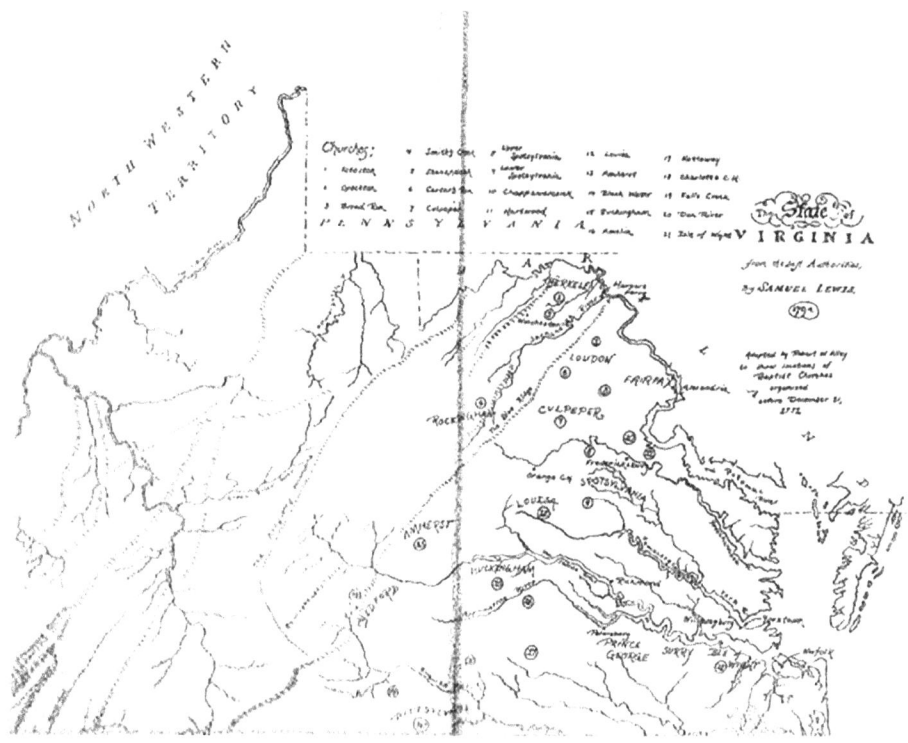

David Barrow
1753-1819

- David Barrow joined the Baptist Church about 1770 in Brunswick County, Virginia where he was born.
- He started preaching the gospel at 18 years of age.
- Ordained around 1772 at 19 years old, he was married the same year.
- He served as minister in Isle of Wight County, Virginia, from 1774 to 1797 at Mill Swamp Baptist Church, Black Creek, and South Quay along with Elder David Mintz. Mill Swamp Church was the "Mother Church" of several churches such as Smithfield, Moore's Swamp, Tucker Swamp, Western Branch, Bethesda and others.
- Barrow served as a soldier in the Revolutionary War.
- In 1779 he and Mintz were visiting a mission church in Nansemond County and were taken to the Nansemond River and dunked and nearly drowned in persecution.
- "Barrow's antislavery conviction was unusual." He freed both his slaves in 1784 and often spoke out thereafter about the evils of slavery. "He became an antislavery activist."
- He served as moderator of the Virginia Portsmouth Association before he moved to Kentucky.
- "He made two preliminary trips to Kentucky and moved there permanently in 1798." Kentucky had "freer climes."

BAPTISTS | 71

- "After a life of twenty odd years' usefulness in Virginia, he moved to Kentucky where he quickly distinguished himself as a man of talents, piety, and usefulness."
- He said he left Virginia "partly because he could not prosper there without slaves."
- He was "an eminent pioneer preacher among the Baptists of Virginia and Kentucky, and a man of great ability, both as a preacher and a writer."
- He served as minister of Mt. Sterling Church in Montgomery County, Kentucky.
- He organized the Kentucky Abolition Society.
- He started a school in 1801 called Lulbegrud School on the Lulbegrud Creek in Montgomery County, Kentucky.
- He exchanged letters with retired President Thomas Jefferson concerning slavery which are a part of Jefferson's records.
- He published a book against slavery.
- He died in Kentucky in 1819.

METHODISTS

John Wesley
(June 28, 1703 - March 2, 1791)

- John Wesley's parents were father Anglican Rector Samuel and mother Susanna. They had nineteen children. John was the fifteenth child. Charles was seventeenth. Thirteen children were buried.
- His father, Samuel, Sr., was a minister of the Church of England, and both grandfathers on mother's side were Puritan ministers.
- Since they were so poor, mother Susanna, homeschooled all the children. She taught Scriptures, principles of right living, and high thinking. She was a very strong influence in his life. "It was her own experience of redemption through Christ that mothered the Methodist revival."
- John's other formal education:
    o Charterhouse School, London (public 1713-1719)
    o Christ Church Oxford (1720)
    o Ordination as Deacon, Oxford in Christ Church (1725)
    o Priest (1728)
    o Fellow of Lincoln College
    o Master of Arts Degree
    o Assisted father at parishes at Epworth and Woods
    o Curate at Wroote
    o Fellow at Oxford until 1729
- Wesley had frequent nosebleeds, which the warm climate in Georgia cured. He was not a well child and adult. He had consumption and tuberculosis.
- His general rules included getting up at 4am, beginning and ending every day with God, following a List of Actions required and behaviors to avoid, and studying of scripture, Hebrew, Greek, French, and German.
- "Defines a Methodist as "one that lives according to the method laid down in the Bible"".
- Neither John nor Charles wanted Methodism to become a dissenting religious sect, but a part of a reformed Church of England.

John Wesley

- He was a part of the "Father of the Holy Club," where four young men gathered together to "Read Bible daily and attend Communion weekly." They also set aside two days each week for fasting and prayer. Charity was later added to activities. The group was started by his brother Charles, William Morgan, George Whitefield, and himself, with others added later.
- He rode horseback preaching on Sundays and ministering to the needy during the week.
- Before the Georgia move, John's religion was one of rules, and doctrine.
- General Oglethorpe founded the Georgia colony in1732 in Savannah.
- In October of 1735, John, his brother Charles, and one other Holy club member, left as missionaries to Georgia, arriving on Feb. 6, 1736.
- He traveled with 26 German Moravians on the Simmonds. A storm raged and the Moravians calmly sang hymns. John was confronted with his own salvation by the Moravian pastor.
- A few days after his arrival in America, John Wesley met the famous Indian Chief Tomochichi of the Yamacraw tribe of the Creek Indian Nation, inspiring "The Great Spirit Meets the Holy Spirit" painting.
- John established schools and an orphanage in Savannah and ministered there. Said he "went to America to convert the Indians, but O! who shall convert me?"
- On December 2, 1737, he left the colony for Carolina and then home after mistakes of judgement.
- Back in England, Wesley recruited George Whitefield to come to America, and their ships passed each other in the Atlantic. Whitefield made seven trips to America.
- Under Moravian encouragement, John found his personal faith. This was followed by a meeting on Aldersgates Street, where he emptied himself and God came in.
- It is said that, "after Aldersgate he was a lion in God's kingdom, who knew no defeat." This was in 1738.
- Eighteen days later at Oxford he preached his famous sermon, "By grace are ye saved through faith."
- Fetter Lane Society was born at a new year's watch night service in 1738-39. George Whitefield was the prime leader after prayer and fasting. He was a great orator.
- Church of England pulpits were closed to their message, so they preached in the open air. They came to be called Wesleyan meetings after John teamed up with George Whitefield.
- Early buildings of Methodism were held by Wesley himself. In London after Bristol, he leased an old foundry building that remodeled seated 1500. John lived above. The first service took place on Sunday Nov 11, 1739, and John preached to five or six thousand. He launched forth in aggressive evangelism. His talent was organization through small classes. He then organized weekly class meetings, and weekly class leaders' meetings. Wesley paid quarterly visits to the classes. He tutored himself to read while on horseback.
- Constantly sought advice from the mother, Susanna.

METHODISTS | 75

- Established lay ministers at the suggestion of his mother. Later she led the way for women preachers.
- The Wesley brothers established Sunday Schools, at their mother's suggestion, and an orphanage in 1742.
- John also established the annual Methodist Conference in 1744 to be the Church's executive backbone.
- The Leed's Conference of 1769 appointed its first preachers to America.
- Methodist Society of England began by meetings in homes.
- In Wesley's lifetime societies started in England, Scotland, Ireland, Wales, and America.
- John Wesley spent 40 years traveling on horseback, more than a quarter of a million miles. He preached 42,000 sermons and wrote more than 200 books.
- John married Mary Vazelle in 1751. They first separated in 1755. She left him in1771.
- In 1782, John Wesley and Thomas Coke started the first tract society.
- John played the flute and Charles played the organ.
- Methodism began as a revival within the Anglican Church in America, as well as in England.
- He died at 88 years of age.
- He remained a member of the Church of England to the end of his life.
- After John died, rulership of the Methodists was to be governed by the Annual Conference of preachers.

Wesley's Vision for Ministry to Native Americans

Charles Wesley
(Dec. 18, 1707 – March 29, 1788) "Father of English Hymns"

Charles Wesley

- Charles was the younger brother of John Wesley by 5 years.
- He entered Oxford University at 19 years of age in 1726.
- He was raised by his other older brother Samuel, an Anglican Priest, after their father died.
- Earnest to save souls and seeing the need for moral living, he started the "Holy Club" at Oxford University in 1729.
- His brother John joined months later along with George Whitefield.
- Charles was ordained quickly before leaving for America.
- In America, Charles was assigned to work at St. Simon Island as Secretary to Governor Oglethorpe, on Feb 6, 1736. He did not get along with Oglethorpe. Oglethorpe later apologized. Charles left America on Aug. 17, 1736. And John remained one more year.
- Back in England Charles experienced a "New Birth" on May 31, 1738 on Pentecost Sunday at Altersgate Church. Three days later his brother John experienced the same.
- Charles preached without notes.
- His message was not welcomed in churches, so he preached out-doors. There was a new renewal group, called "Methodists," within the Church of England.
- Charles preached to thousands. In five years (1739-1743), he reached 149,400 people.
- In addition to his preaching, he produced 56 volumes of hymns. Charles wrote hymns and his brother John edited and produced hymn books.
- In 1749, Charles married Sally Gwynne. They are believed to have been happy in their marriage. Three of their children survived to adulthood.
- Evangelism and music were a large part of Methodism.
- Charles formed a partnership for ministry with his brother John.
- Charles served in ministry for 50 years, from 1738-1788.
- About 6,500 to 9,000 hymns (some 31 versus long!) were written by Charles, including:
    - Hark the Herald Angels Sing
    - Christ the Lord is Risen Today
    - Amazing Love, And Can it be that I Should Gain
    - O for a Thousand Tongues to Sing
    - Love Divine
    - Jesus, Lover of my Soul
    - Rejoice the Lord is King
    - Come, thou Long Expected Jesus
    - And many more

George Whitefield (Whitfield)

(December 16, 1714 – September 30, 1770)

"He planted evangelism in America"
"America's Spiritual Founding Father"

- George Whitefield was the youngest of seven children born to Thomas and Elisabeth Whitefield, in Bell Inn in Gloucester, England which they owned. Thomas died when George was two, and his mother left George's step-father when George was six.
- He attended The Crypt School, where he expressed an early talent for acting and theater, while acting stories from the Bible.
- Whitefield enrolled at Pembroke College, Oxford University in 1732, with Granter free tuition).
- In 1735, he joined the "Holy Club" and experienced spiritual "New Birth," three years before the Wesleys' experiences at Aldersgate.
- That year he took over leadership of the "Holy Club" after John and Charles Wesley left for America.
- He was ordained in 1736 as a deacon in the Church of England at Gloucester. And in January of 1739, he was ordained into priesthood at Oxford.
- That year he began preaching outdoors to large crowds because the Anglian Church (COE) would not allow him to preach.
- Whitefield split from the Wesley brothers for a short period of time over doctrine, but this split did not last.
- On November 14, 1741 he married widow Elizabeth James. She died of fever August 9, 1768. Their son died at 4 months. She had 4 miscarriages.
- Whitefield initially denounced slavery but changed his mind. In 1748-50 he campaigned for slavery after seeing the need for it to financially sustain the orphanage. Slavery was legalized in Georgia in 1751.
- Whitefield had charisma, a loud voice, small stature, and cross-eyed appearance.
- Whitefield used printed material, advanced men for preaching visits, published sermons, and advanced advertisement of revivals.
- He became very famous and well known internationally on both sides of the Atlantic Ocean.
- Benjamin Franklin heard Whitefield in Philadelphia, PA. Franklin calculated by Whitefield's voice that he could be heard by 30,000 people in open air. The two became

lifelong friends. They started an orphanage for boys, Charity School, which became Academy of Philadelphia (1751), then in 1755 the College of Philadelphia. Both were predecessors of the University of Pennsylvania. Whitefield's statue still stands on the campus.

Benjamin Franklin
Friend, Publicist,
Publisher of Whitefield

- Whitfield County, Georgia was named for him.
- Whitefield is honored together with Francis Asbury with a feast day on the liturgical calendar of the Episcopal Church (USA) on November 15.
- In 1753, Whitefield started publishing hymnals.
- He ministered for 34 years, delivering over 18,000 sermons, to an audience of up to 10 million people in England and America. He published 78 sermons.
- When died he left everything in Georgia to Countess Huntington, including 4000 acres of land and 50 slaves.
- He was the true founder of evangelicalism. And one of the founders of Methodism and the evangelical movement.
- He remained an Anglican priest with the Church of England.
- Whitefield made 15 journeys to Scotland, 2 to Ireland, 1 to Bermuda, Gibraltar, Netherlands, and Portugal.
- He was the "First internationally famous itinerant preacher and first modern transatlantic celebrity of any kind."

Whitefield Took Seven Trips to America

1ST TRIP: May – August, 1738

- George went to Savannah, Georgia as a parish priest. He also served as Colonial chaplain in Savannah, and the orphanage founded by Gen. Oglethorpe. He left for England from Charleston, South Carolina.

2ND TRIP : 1739-1741

- George arrived in Philadelphia aboard the *Elizabeth,* on November 2, 1739. There he met Benjamin Franklin and they became friends for 31 years. He received advanced publicity from Franklin's newspapers.
- He led a twofold ministry, preaching while he built the Bethesda orphanage in Leigh Valley, PA with the Moravian Brethren.
- He traveled horseback from New York City to Charleston.
- **On December 16, 1739 he preached at Bruton Parish in Williamsburg, Virginia, however, the plantations were too far apart to get crowds.**
- He preached in Edenton, North Carolina on December 20.

- He visited Bath, NC 4 times during his career.
- He spent Christmas in New Bern, NC and New Year's Day of 1740 in Charleston, SC.
- He canoed to Savannah, GA to visit the orphanage and the church, located between Charleston and Savannah.
- He traveled by sea to Phila in April 1740.
- In July he took a ship back to Savannah and Charleston.
- In August he sailed to New England via Newport, Rhode Island.
- He arrived in Boston on September 18, and on September 27 he preached to 15,000 at Boston Commons, and then Old South Church on October 8. From there he went West to Northampton, Connecticut and visited with Jonathan Edwards. In November he went to Yale College, then back to NY, Staten Island, and Newark, NJ. Again he went to Phila., NJ, MD, DEL, and then South, possibly via VA, then South to Charleston, SC.
- In October 1740, he preached in New England. There he met Jonathan Edwards and studied Calvin's theology. He started preaching predestination. He was part of the "Great Awakening" New England revival in 1740. He included enslaved people in his revivals.
- He left in January 1741 for England.

*George married Elizabeth James from Wales on November 14, 1741. England and France were at war, delaying his return to America.

3ʳᴰ TRIP: 1744 – 1748

- In August 1744, George, in poor health, sailed on the *Wilmington* with his wife Elizabeth. They were accompanied by William Seward, his publicist.
- On October 26, 1744 they landed in York, Maine. George was very sick.
- By November they had reached Boston. Whitefield was in New England for 9 months preaching. He and his wife were also hosted by Jonathan Edwards and wife in Connecticut.
- Next they went to New York City and Philadelphia.
- In fall of 1745 he traveled south through Maryland and **Virginia** to check on the Bethesda orphanage.
- In Hanover County, VA, in October, Samuel Morris, earlier converted by reading Whitefield's sermons, held home meetings, and built a meetinghouse. This started a great move of God.
- On November 8, 1745 he arrived with his wife in Charleston, SC. For 6 months he shuttled back and forth between Charleston and Bethesda, working to get the orphanage on a better footing.
- He left Charleston in May 1746 for Philadelphia.
- The summer of 1746 had Whitefield preaching several weeks in MD and then to southern colonies, like Charleston and Bethesda, until 1747.

- In 1747, Elizabeth wanted to go back to England after another miscarriage. Whitefield purchased a 640 acre plantation in SC called Providence.
- Whitefield returned to Philadelphia in May 1747 where, after the 400 mile journey, he preached 30 times.
- During the summer of 1747, he took a northern tour through New York City, Boston, and as far north as York, Maine.
- In Charleston, he preached meetings intended for Negros.
- He left for Bermuda on May 1, 1748. His wife Elizabeth waited for him in Charleston. She enjoyed the weather there.
- He arrived in England without his wife. She came later in June 1749.

4TH TRIP: 1751-1752

- Whitefield arrived in Georgia in August 1751 to check on Bethesda orphanage.
- Elizabeth did not go as she had another miscarriage.
- During this trip he divested himself of Providence plantation.
- His mother died in February 1752, and he then left Charleston for England.

5TH TRIP: 1754- 1755

- Whitefield traveled in May 1754 to SC and Bethesda orphanage via Lisbon, Portugal. He brought 12 orphans with him from England.
- He spent eight weeks in the South, the sailed to Philadelphia and New York City.
- Beginning in October 1754 in New England, he preached 100 times in 8 weeks.
- **In January 1755 Whitefield spent a week ministering to Presbyterian churches in Richmond, VA. "In Virginia the prospects very promising," he said.**
- In March 1755, he left for England. The Seven Year War, as well as the French and Indian War with the British prevented his return to America for several years.

6TH TRIP: 1763 -1765

- Whitefield traveled the East Coast for a year and 9 months.
- **On August 24, 1763 he went to Virginia and traveled plantation to plantation. Once in Northern Neck and Petersburg, he "Kept up the spark of the revival there and in a few other places."**
- He went to Philadelphia in November 1764.
- In February 1764, he returned to New England, via Long Island and Boston.
- He traveled overland south to Georgia, stopped along the way in New Bern, NC. He was in poor health at this time.
- He was in Charleston in November 1764.
- From December 1764 to February 1765 he was in Bethesda, Georgia.

- **He met Patrick Henry May 20, 1765 in Petersburg, VA, in person to discuss their mutual opposition to the Stamp Act.**
- He then sailed to New York.
- He sailed for England on June 10, 1765.
- Back in England, on February 13, 1766 he supported Benjamin Franklin's testimony in the House of Commons against the Stamp Act.

7TH TRIP: 1769 – 1770

- On Sept 4, 1769 Whitefield arrived in Charleston with Cornelius Winter and Richard Smith. From there he canoed to Bethesda.
- He spent the winter in Georgia.
- In April 1770, he traveled through the colonies by coastal vessel to Philadelphia, and then on to Albany, NY. By September he was in Boston.
- On September 23 he was in Portsmouth, NH.
- On September 29 he traveled from Exeter to Newberryport, Massachusetts.
- After 34 years in ministry, Whitefield preached his last sermon at Old South Presbyterian Church, Newberryport, Mass., the day before he died September 30, 1770, at age 56. He was buried at the same church. John Wesley preached his funeral in England Nov 18, 1770.

George Whitefield on Slavery

- Whitefield wrote that the "Providence of God has appointed this colony rather for the work of black slaves than for Europeans, because of the hot climate, to which the Negroes are better used than white people."
- He took a great interest in the Bethesda orphanage, outside Savannah Georgia, that John Wesley had started.
    1. He "showed great concern for the plight of the slaves in America."
    2. He "emphasized the necessity of Christian evangelism among Blacks."
    3. He was called "the first great friend of the American negro."
    4. He stressed the need for education of the Negros, and their being taught reading, writing, and being baptized. He pushed for the civility of their treatment.
    5. He preached to masters of slaves about the living conditions and mistreatment of slaves but stopped short of moral judgement.
    6. He had a dilemma at the Bethesda orphanage in 1747 with mismanagement of white help. Georgia made having slaves illegal. He felt that Bethesda could not function without black labor.
    7. In South Carolina slavery was legal. "South Carolina modeled its system of slavery after the island of Barbados which had a reputation of harshness."

8. Whitefield bought a plantation in South Carolina and became a slaveholder.
9. In 1748 he was openly agitating for the legalization of slavery in Georgia in the name of "altruistic ends" and "economics."
10. He established a school for black people in Charleston with Jonathan Bryan, a converted slaveholder of SC, and a friend of Whitefield's.
11. He wrote to the enslaved converts a letter called "Letter to the Negroes" welcoming them, using Ephesians 2:9, Colossians 3:11, and John 10:16 as references. He addresses them as "My Dear Brethren in CHRIST, the glorious Head of the Church." He tells them the benefits that await converts, and the responsibilities of their new status.
12. Whitefield deeded the "buildings, lands, Negroes, books, furniture," "and all other possessions there to the Countess of Huntingdon." After her death Georgia officials took custody of the property.
13. Whitefield was like "Thomas Jefferson, Patrick Henry, James Madison and others—who preached liberty and human equality but did not liberate their own slaves."
14. Phillis Wheatley, a slave girl, owned by an evangelical family in Boston, wrote an elegy poem to Whitefield on his death titled "On the Death of the Reverend George Whitefield." She would later "publicly criticize American slavery" "but she only praised Whitefield and His Savior."

On the Death of the Rev. George Whitefield, 1770
By Phillis Wheatley

Hail, happy saint, on thine immortal throne,
Possest of glory, life, and bliss unknown;
We hear no more the music of thy tongue,
Thy wonted auditories cease to throng.
Thy sermons in unequall'd accents flow'd,
And ev'ry bosom with devotion glow'd;
Thou didst in strains of eloquence refin'd
Inflame the heart, and captivate the mind.
Unhappy we the setting sun deplore,
So glorious once, but ah! it shines no more.
Behold the prophet in his tow'ring flight!
He leaves the earth for heav'n's unmeasur'd height,
And worlds unknown receive him from our sight.
There Whitefield wings with rapid course his way,
And sails to Zion through vast seas of day.

Phillis Wheatley

Thy pray'rs, great saint, and thine incessant cries
Have pierc'd the bosom of thy native skies.
Thou moon hast seen, and all the stars of light,
How he has wrestled with his God by night.
He pray'd that grace in ev'ry heart might dwell,
He long'd to see America excell;
He charg'd its youth that ev'ry grace divine
Should with full lustre in their conduct shine;
That Saviour, which his soul did first receive,
The greatest gift that ev'n a God can give,
He freely offer'd to the num'rous throng,
That on his lips with list'ning pleasure hung.
"Take him, ye wretched, for your only good,
"Take him ye starving sinners, for your food;
"Ye thirsty, come to this life-giving stream,
"Ye preachers, take him for your joyful theme;
"Take him my dear Americans, he said,
"Be your complaints on his kind bosom laid:
"Take him, ye Africans, he longs for you,
"Impartial Saviour is his title due:
"Wash'd in the fountain of redeeming blood,
"You shall be sons, and kings, and priests to God."
Great Countess, we Americans revere
Thy name, and mingle in thy grief sincere;
New England deeply feels, the Orphans mourn,
Their more than father will no more return.
But, though arrested by the hand of death,
Whitefield no more exerts his lab'ring breath,
Yet let us view him in th' eternal skies,
Let ev'ry heart to this bright vision rise;
While the tomb safe retains its sacred trust,
Till life divine re-animates his dust.

Francis Asbury
(August 20 or 21, 1745 - March 31, 1816)

"…is entitled to rank as one of the builders of our nation."
President Calvin Coolidge
at Dedication of Asbury on His Horse statue in Washington, D.C.

- Francis Asbury was a Christian abolitionist and revivalist.
- His parents were Joseph and Elizabeth (Eliza) Rogers Asbury.
- His father Joseph was a farm labor, gardener, and later worked at a brewery. His mother Eliza was Welsh.
- Methodism was central to Eliza's spiritual awakening after depression because of her daughter's death. She invited "any people who had the appearance of religion to her home."
- Francis "Frank" was born near Hamstead Bridge in West Midlands, England.
- His education included:

Francis Ashbury

   - A free school at Sneal's Green. A cruel schoolmaster forced Francis to leave school at 12 or 13.
   - He learned metalworker and spent six and a half years in the trade.
   - He was an avid reader.
   - He joined Methodist class meetings.
   - At about 17 he began exhorting and preaching in public.
- At age 21 Francis took the place of a traveling preacher assigned to the Staffordshire Circuit.
- For four years Wesley assigned Asbury to rural circuits in the South of England.
- In August 1771, at 26, he volunteered at the Bristol Conference to go to America. He answered Wesley's call for volunteers.
- He arrived in Philadelphia October 27, 1771.
- He understood the common man and could relate to the people. Most Americans lived on farms and in small villages.
- "Asbury accepted that America was culturally different from England, with its own set of needs."
- He related more to the South's Methodism than the North's, and their loudness in worship.
- By May 1774 most of the Methodists' gains were in the South.
- Asbury spent 10 years in Maryland, Delaware, and Virginia, "where Methodism took shape in the fires of revival."

- The Revolutionary War started on April 19, 1775. Wesley ordered Asbury home to England. Asbury refused. He stayed neutral and did not take sides like Wesley.
- Asbury heard of the Virginia Revival which started in 1763 by Anglian Priest Rev. Devereux Jarrett in Dinwiddie, Virginia, and wanted to see for himself. **He arrived in Norfolk for the first time on May 29, 1775.** He was in Portsmouth in October, and Brunswick Circuit, as well as 14 other counties.
- The Virginia Revival included the Church of England, Methodist, and Presbyterian worshipers falling, crying, and shouting under their conviction. This was labeled "Southern Zeal." Reported crowds in 1775 were between 2,000 and 3,000 at Methodist meetings. These revivals created the model for Methodist expansion for 40 years. Also, Methodists started weekly home group meetings which became a part of Methodism and discipleship training.
- Asbury focused Methodism on evangelistic doctrine, practices, lifestyle, and purposes… "live religion", "scripture based and hymns sung, and proclaimed the human ability to respond to God's grace."
- The Church of England was disestablished in the South of America in 1776 to 1780's,
- (MD, VA, GA, NC, SC) ending Tax support for churches.
- Thomas Rankin was sent by Wesley in 1773 to lead the American Methodists.
- Asbury stayed in Maryland in 1777, and in Delaware starting February 1778 for 2 and a half years because of the war. Rankin, American Methodist Superintendent, returned to England in March 1778.
- **In 1780, starting in May, Asbury traveled through Virginia, then North Carolina, and returned to Virginia in August. "In Nansemond County, Virginia, he preached to 300 people with "uncommon freedom."**
- In 1781 Asbury started going South in the winter, and North in the summer.
- In 1784 John Wesley named Asbury and Thomas Coke "superintendents" of work in America.
- Asbury was appointed in September 1783, General Assistant by Wesley, as the highest ranking Methodist in America. Asbury had kept North and South Methodist leadership together. In 1784 Asbury was still paid only $60 a year, plus traveling expenses.
- In 1788 John Wesley rebuked Asbury and Coke for calling themselves "Bishops".
- By 1788 Asbury expanded the Methodist annual conference to include 8 district conferences.
- Methodists in America changed their name to Methodist Episcopal Church (MEC) to differentiate themselves from England and to show alliance with the Church of England.
- Asbury continued the conferences in America annually, supervised by a bishop.
- Quarterly meeting of circuits. These meetings grew into camp meetings for food, fellowship, preaching, and bringing one's own provisions for sleeping instead of being assigned to homes.

- Camp meetings in America started around the 1790's and continued into the late 1800's. Camp meetings started in 1800 in Virginia in Brunswick County, and they "appealed to Asbury because of their fervor and the enthusiasm with which his preaching was greeted."
- Asbury (MEC) stressed weekly class meetings with a leader organized into circuits.
- Asbury ordained Richard Allen, the first black deacon, in 1799.
- Richard Allen (1760 – 1831), a former slave, began a career as a teaching Methodist after purchasing his freedom. He was licensed to preach in 1784 by Methodist. In 1794 Allen founded "Mother Bethel" church in Philadelphia.
- "former slave Richard Allen preached the gospel as a Methodist circuit-riding companion of former slave owner Freeborn Garrettson."
- In 1816 Allen began the African Methodist Episcopal Church (AME).

Bishop Richard Allen

- Asbury promoted separating religious leadership from wealth and formal education. He used poverty to keep himself honest.
- Asbury became a personal friend of Thomas Jefferson.
- Asbury ordained over 2000 to 3000 Methodist preachers.
- Asbury had ridden over 130,000 miles by horse, despite poor health. He crossed the Allegheny Mountains some sixty times.
- He likely delivered more than 10,000 to 12,000 sermons.
- He preached his last sermon on March 24, 1816 in Richmond, Va.
- He died on March 31, 1816 in Spotsylvania, VA and was buried May 10, 1816 in Baltimore, MD., at Eutaw Street Church.

Francis Asbury on Horseback

- Asbury never married, had no children, did not own a home, staying instead with families.
- A statue of Asbury on his horse stands in Washington, DC. President Calvin Coolidge in his dedication speech said that Asbury "is entitled to rank as one of the builders of our nation."
- "Asbury's last letter was written in Virginia, the state which has seen more of his travels than any other state." – Asbury Journal Vol. III, p. 556

Maps Show Examples of Asbury Visits in Virginia

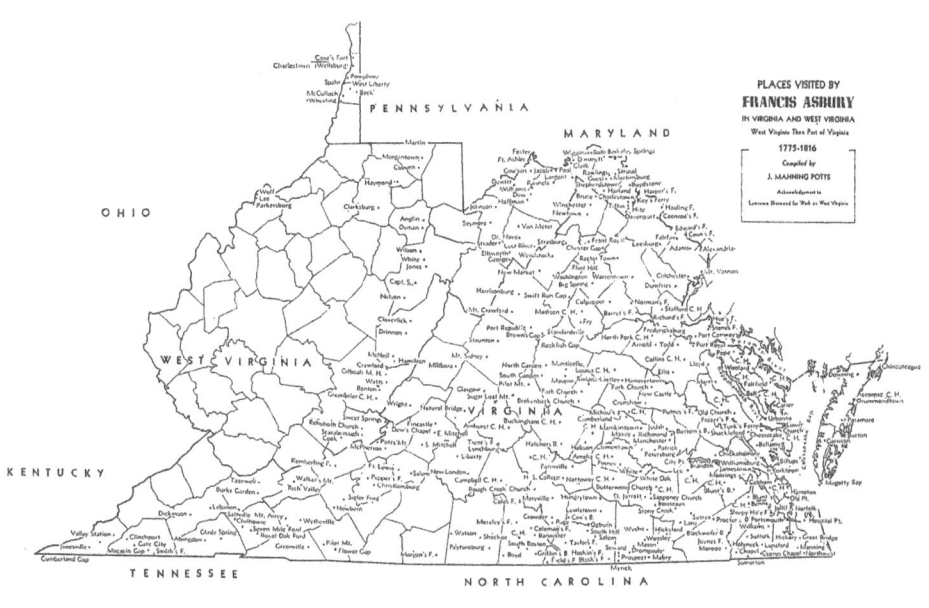

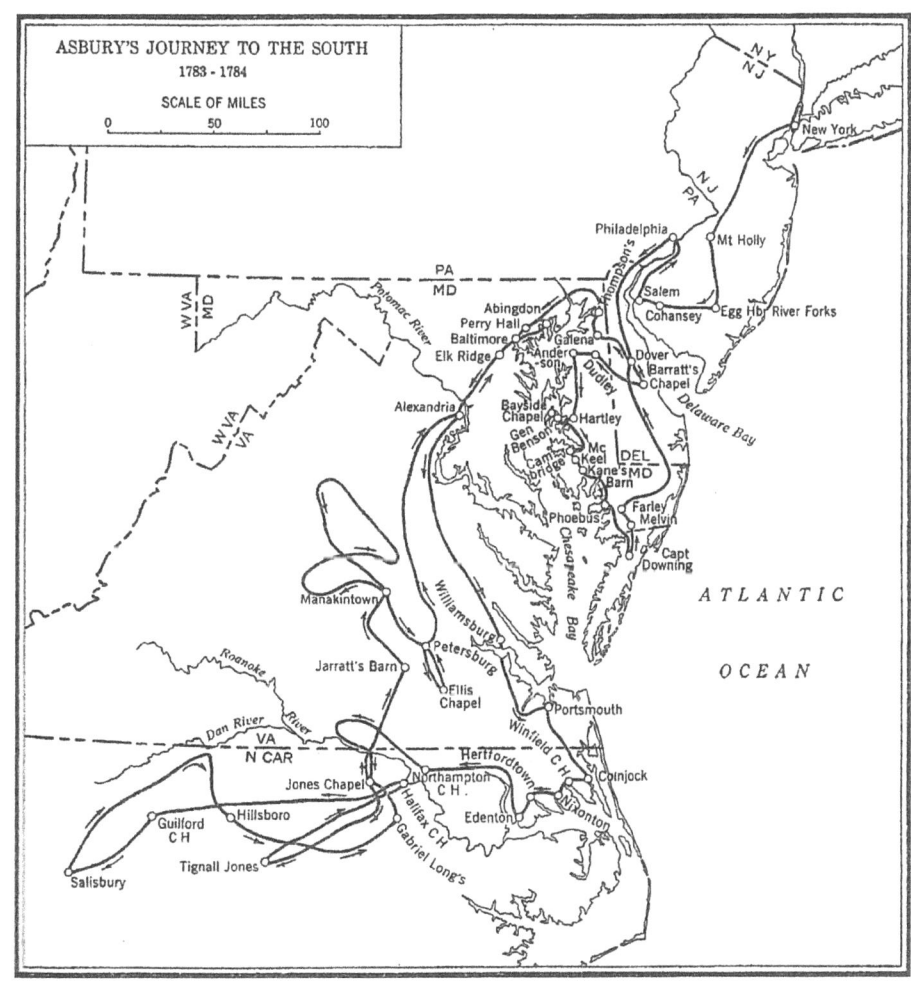

OTHER VIRGINIA METHODISTS

Reverend Robert Williams
(Unknown – 1775)
First Methodist Minister to Come to Virginia

- Robert Williams was a local preacher from Ireland who began to travel in 1766 with the Irish Conference. He was born in England and later moved to Ireland.
- In 1769 Williams spoke to Wesley indicating his desire to go to America.
- In September 1769 Williams arrived in NY with John Wesley's consent.
- Early in 1772, May 29, Williams landed by ship in Norfolk after strong winds. The ship was bound for Baltimore but winds caused the ship to put in at Norfolk. He had only "a pair of saddle-bags, containing a few pieces of clothing, a loaf of bread, and a bottle of milk."
- In Norfolk, "Standing on the courthouse, he began to sing. The people gathered around, attracted by the unusual proceeding, and wondering what it meant. After singing, the preacher prayed. He then announced his text, and, in old Methodist fashion, warned them to flee from the wrath of God, and be saved from their sins."
- He then went to Portsmouth.
- Williams was the first Methodist to visit southern Virginia. Joseph Pilmoor, another preacher, landed later in July 1772 and formed the first Methodist society in Portsmouth in November of that year.
- In October 1772 he revisited Norfolk with William Watters.
- Norfolk and Portsmouth were called the "cradle of Methodism in the South."
- He would use the many courthouse steps, sing hymns, kneeling for prayer, and preach. The same as John Wesley used in England.
- In 1773, William's visited in Petersburg the Anglican clergyman Devereux Jarratt, leader of the Great Awakening in Virginia. Revival started in Dinwiddie County at Bath Parish where Jarratt was the Rector.

Robert Williams

- Williams was the first Methodist contact with Jarratt. Jarratt wrote to John Wesley of his favorable impression of Williams, who was evangelical in his delivery of the message of the gospel.
- William was the first Methodist preacher to come into the Petersburg area in February 1773.
- Williams caught new inspiration from Jarratt. "a most wonderful revival broke out. The flame soon extended over into North Carolina."
- He went preaching into the northern part of NC.
- His simple devotion and earnest evangelical preaching had stirred many. His tears in public, dealing with people one by one, questioning them about the welfare of their souls, etc.
- At the first Methodist Conference in America, held in Philadelphia, July 1, 1773, Robert Williams was assigned to Petersburg as an itinerant preacher.
- Williams married in May 1774. He stopped traveling as an itinerant, and preached only locally.
- In 1774 Williams organized the first Methodist circuit in VA, which extended from Petersburg beyond to Roanoke and into NC, and eastward to Norfolk and Portsmouth. The second circuit was the Norfolk Circuit.
- Williams started printing and circulating books, tracks, Wesley pamphlets and conference data, as well as Wesley's sermons.
- Rev. Williams is thought to have preached the first Methodist sermon in Suffolk.
- In April 1775, Williams carried news of revival in Virginia to Francis Asbury in Philadelphia.
- At a Philadelphia, PA conference Williams reported 500 to 600 souls justified by faith in Virginia, and 5 or 6 new circuits formed. The Conference assigned Williams to the Brunswick Circuit in 1775.
- Williams lived long enough to witness results of his labors in the outbreak of the great revival 1775-76.
- Asbury mentioned in his Journal, July 26, 1775, and again Aug 8th, that he visited Williams and his wife living on a farm on the Portsmouth-Suffolk road (in Nansemond County).
- Williams died Sept 26, 1775. He and his wife were living in Nansemond County, off the public road between Portsmouth to Suffolk.
- Francis Asbury preached his funeral and burial, Sept 28, 1775. "Perhaps no one in America has been an instrument of awaking so many souls, as God has awakened by him."
- Thomas Rankin and Francis Asbury were made executors of Robert Williams's will.
- Asbury Journals mentioned he stayed with widow Williams, Oct 30th 1775, and the next day preached at the Suffolk Court House.

Bishop William McKendree
(1757 - Unknown)
First American born Methodist Bishop
Methodist Conference

- William McKendree was born July 6, 1757 in King William County, VA.
- He was called to ministry under Methodist revivalist John Easter of Brunswick Circuit in VA, where revival fires burned.
- One year after his conversion, McKendree was admitted in trial as an itinerant preacher.
- He was mentored by Anglican Devereux Jarratt in Dinwiddie County, a revivalist working with the Methodist.
- He traveled extensively with Francis Asbury, developed, and preached with him. The two men developed a close friendship.
- McKendree was part of the "Great Awakening in VA."

Bishop William McKendree

- On January 20, 1782 he visited Asbury at the "Nansemond Great Preaching House" in Chuckatuck. He met up with Asbury at White Oak Chapel (Anglican Jarratt's in Dinwiddie County).
- 1782 saw the first Virginia Conference.
- In November 1785 McKendree dined with Asbury at General Roberdeau's (who later introduced Asbury and Coke to General Washington).
- For a short time he was assigned and worked with James O'Kelly. But he ultimately chose to travel with Asbury.
- He had a 12 year circuit in VA, then went on to Kentucky and Tennessee in 1800, where he served eight more years. He was the dominant leader west of the mountains.
- In 1808 he held the first Methodist Conference in TN.
- In 1808 the General Conference in Baltimore elected McKendree a Bishop, making him the first native born American to occupy that high office.
- McKendree preached at "Light Street Church on the first Sunday he made the walls of the old church to ring with his powerful voice and overwhelmed the congregation with his eloquence. "Multitudes fell helpless from their seats as if shot with a rifle" and an "electric influence thrilled through every heart," while the sermon closed with "a sweet and holy influence, like the mellow light of Indian Summer."
- On February 20,1815 he presided over the Lynchburg, VA Conference. This was the last VA Conference Asbury attended.
- He was a confirmed bachelor.

- When Asbury died March 31, 1816 in Spotsylvania County in VA. McKendree was the officiating minister and gave the funeral oration May 10, 1816 at Eutow Street Church in Baltimore. McKendree was the only surviving bishop.
- Asbury willed all his earthly possessions to McKendree including horse, clothing, and books, including Asbury's Hebrew Bible.
- In March1817, he wrote a bio of Asbury and presented it to the General Conference.
- "Listed as one of the heroes of Virginia Methodist's first 100 years, Robert Williams, Francis Asbury, George Shadford, Edward Dromgoole, Jesse Lee, William McKendree, Slith Mead,…." said Dr. William Bennett, President of Randolph-Macon College, at the one hundredth anniversary of the Virginia Methodist Conference, in 1882.

Timeline - Early Methodists

Early Methodists
Each Remained an Anglican Priest Until Death

1700　1710　1720　1730　1740　1750　1760　1770　1780　1790　1800　1810

John Wesley

June 28, 1703 - March 2, 1791

Savannah, GA
1736-37

Charles Wesley

Dec 18, 1707 - March 29, 1788

Savannah, GA
1736

George Whitefield

Dec 16, 1714 - Sep 30, 1770

Made Seven Trips to America
(1) 1738
(2) 1739-41
(3) 1744-48
(4) 1751-52
(5) 1754-55
(6) 1763-65
(7) 1769-70

Francis Asbury

Aug 20, 1745 - March 31, 1816

America
1771 - 1816

METHODIST AND VIRGINIA NATIVE AMERICANS TODAY

Like John Wesley and his brother Charles, who came to Savannah, Georgia in 1736 to minister to the Indians, the United Methodist Church (UMC) continues to minister to Native Americans.

Many annual Methodist conferences have a Committee of Native American Ministries which seeks to advocate for ministry with and by Native Americans and to share the diverse culture, history, and tradition of Native people.

Native American Ministry Sunday is designated on the third Sunday of Easter. An offering across the globe is taken to support Native Americans.

The Ministry supports tribes all over the country, including 573 Federally recognized tribes, and also has ministries on Indian reservations.

UMC also supports 150 Native American congregations.

Native American Seminary Award is given at Duke Divinity School.

CONTINUED INFLUENCE (VIRGINIA TRIBES)

Nansemond Indian Tribe

The Nansemond Tribe was documented by John Smith as existing in several towns south of Jamestown on the River in Virginia now called the Nansemond River. It had 1200 members in the 1600's, and by the early 1700's surviving members became Christians and lived around the Dismal Swamp. In 1850 the Methodist organized a mission church and built it between the Seaboard and Virginia Railroads at Bowers Hill. After the American Civil War, a one room school was built at the same site for the tribal Indian children. It was used from the 1890s to 1928. Indian children could not attend white schools and were not welcomed at black schools.

Indiana UMC church still exists at the same location.

Indiana Methodist Church 1850, and school 1890

Rappahannock Indian Tribe

John Smith mapped in the 1600's fourteen (14) Rappahannock villages on the north side of what is now called Rappahannock River. The south side of the river was the tribe's hunting grounds. They were later driven in-land, off the river, to a place called Indian Neck, which is near Tappahannock, Virginia.

Chief G. Anne Richardson's Story

In 1994, my Tribe began a series of community meetings to seek solutions to the loss of tribal traditions because our elders were dying at such an increased rate. When one tribal elder dies the community can lose its history, its family genealogies, traditional ways and spiritual beliefs because they are oral history societies. These elders keep the stories and wisdom of their people and someone once said; "the loss of one elder in a Tribe is equal to the burning of the Library at Alexandria." We began planning how we would capture and protect what we had left of our traditional knowledge and ways as a community. We decided that we desperately needed a Tribal Center where these ways could be recorded and taught to future generations. The result of the meetings was a plan for the uses of the building. I sought a young Native man trained in draft and design and asked him to draft a design based on what we needed. We began the Project with a small grant to put in a well and began the structure. As we began the work, God started sending "Volunteers in Missions" from the Ashland District United Methodist Churches. Patricia Koontz's, their Chair, led the way and she became my best and trusted friend. They began coming in teams and helping us to raise the funds for supplies along the way. It was a miracle to behold everyday as I gave up my job upon God's instruction to work daily to build this Center. Others from the Tribe came to take care of the administrative, construction and project management duties that were arising from all the work. I began going into Methodist churches speaking on the Project to raise funds and recruit volunteers. Our people couldn't believe these Non-Native people would come and love us enough to help us build a Tribal Center. Upon collecting documents for our archives, we found that the Methodist Church from the Ashland District had assisted our community in the 1800's to build our first church and school. The documents said, our revival services lasted an entire week and their worship was so loud that they disturbed our country neighbors a mile away. I began telling this to the churches I would visit and before long, I was getting calls from all over the Methodist community. In the process, God built in me the desire to destroy the walls that had before divided us. He began

Chief G. Anne Richardson

to teach me about the power of reconciliation. I began to understand how the Methodist hadn't wanted to change who we were, they didn't see us as inferior, they just wanted to teach us about Jesus. They supported our community in the 1800's by training and ordaining our own ministers.

Satan had erected walls to keep us apart because of the power we had when we came together with our knowledge of the spirit realm and the Methodists' knowledge of Jesus! I always say, I started constructing a building, and in the process God built me into a minister for Him, a leader for my people and a warrior for both.

As we began to build the archives or documents for our Tribe, we found minutes to tribal meetings held in 1921 where they had planned a building for exactly the same uses we had identified during our meetings in 1994. Then we found minutes from tribal meetings held in 1970 planning a building for the same uses. Funds had been raised by the Tribe in 1970 and we purchased 1000 blocks to start the building, however for lack of funds, the Project stopped there. Uncovering these 1000 blocks which had been carefully covered and stored for future use, when we tested them they were like new so those were used as the foundation stones for the first building in 1995. The Tribal Center was completed in 1997 as a six thousand square foot community building complete with kitchen, dining room, auditorium, classrooms and offices. What a journey for my people, being reconnected with the Methodist church and finding the love of others through Jesus Christ.

Rappahannock Tribal Center Today

PART IV

Great Awakening in Virginia 1740-1790

"As soon as it began, the power of the Lord came down on the assembly like a rushing mighty wind, and it seemed as if the whole house was filled with the presence of God. A flame kindled and ran from heart to heart. Many were deeply convinced of sin; many mourners were filled with consolation; and many believers were so overwhelmed with love that they could not doubt but God had enabled them to love Him with all their heart."

REVEREND DEVEREUX JARRATT, ANGLICAN PRIEST

GREAT AWAKENINGS IN VIRGINIA

Overview

The Great Awakening of Virginia was primarily a revival of personal religion, which made for the betterment of society. The awakening brought unity in the spirit and in the denominations that prepared Virginia for the Revolutionary War which led to complete religious liberty.

"Not only was the Great Awakening an intercolonial movement; it was part of a larger awakening within the whole British Empire, which may very properly be called the Methodist Revival."

Timeline - Revivals in America

Revivals in America											
1700	1710	1720	1730	1740	1750	1760	1770	1780	1790	1800	1810
		1720s — German/ Dutch Reformers in NY, NJ, PA, VA									
				1735-41 — New England Great Awakening with Jonathan Edwards							
				1740-90 — Great Awakening in Virginia							

German Reformers and Dutch Reformers (Mennonite)
1720's Down the Shenandoah Valley from the Germantown, PA, Mennonite Revival

- German Reformers (Mennonites) in Germantown, PA, had a revival starting in 1722-1726 that also came down the Shenandoah Valley in VA. It affected Lutherans, Morovians, Brethren, and German Evangelicals.
- Theodurus Frelinghuysen, a German, an apostle of revivalism with the Dutch Reformers, arrived in 1720 in NY. Revival broke out in NY, NJ, and down the Shenandoah Valley in Virginia. It spread to other German Reformers, ie. Moravians, and to the Lutherans.
- George Whitfield came to the NJ area as an apostle of the Great Awakening in 1739 and 1740. He preached to thousands outdoors. The "revival spirit tended to break down denominational exclusiveness." Whitefield also preached to a crowd at Germantown, PA that numbered about 5,000.

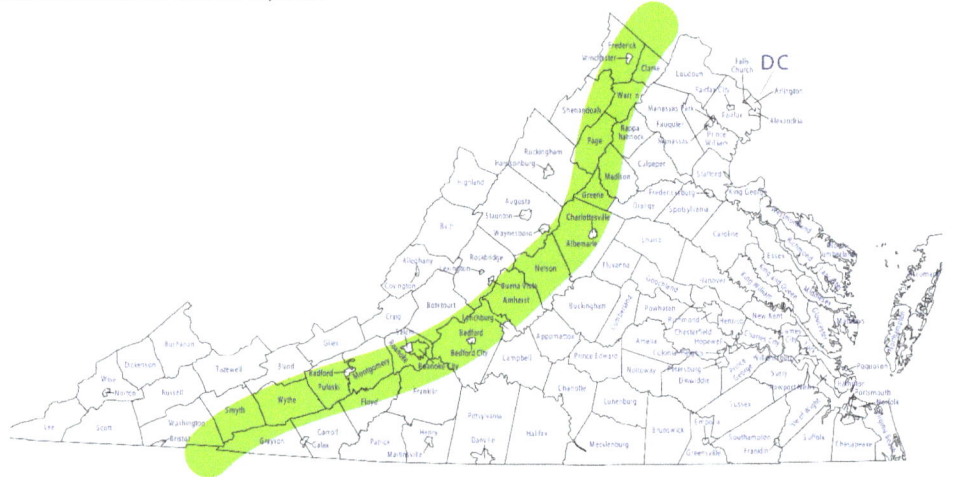

Early German Reformers and Dutch Reformers Revivals in Virginia

- German/Dutch Reformers Revival 1720's in NY and NJ.
- From Germantown, PA, down the Shenandoah Valley, 1726.
- Includes Mennonites, Lutherans, Brethren, and Morovians (who settled in NC)

GREAT AWAKENINGS IN VIRGINIA | 105

Presbyterian

1740 – 1758 Hanover County Revival with Samuel Morris and Samuel Davis

Samuel Davis

- George Whitefield, Anglican evangelistic minister, visited Virginia five times as a Methodist missionary evangelist. The first visit Whitefield preached in 1739 at Bruton Parish in Williamsburg, with the Governor in attendance. His sermon, "What Think Ye of Christ," was published in the Gazette. Samuel Morris, a Presbyterian bricklayer in Hanover County, started reading Whitefield's sermon aloud to others in his home. Meetings outgrew the home and he set up the "Morris's Reading House." Morris started being invited to other areas to read the sermons. Revival broke out.
- On Whitefield's third visit to Virginia in 1745, he rekindled this revival in the Hanover, VA, area with five days of preaching.
- Samuel Davis came to the Hanover County area in the late 1740's, and had a struggle getting licenses in the various counties. But he persevered. "He found people eager for the evangelical doctrines…" "The chief aim of his preaching was to promote genuine Christianity by changing hearts and lives of men."
- He was the "earliest hymn writer of Colonial Presbyterianism", and an eloquent preacher. Davis was preaching open air revivals as far as Lancaster and Northumberland Counties, and other parts of the Northern Neck. Whitefield's fifth visit to America in January 1755, gave fresh breath to the Presbyterian revival in the Richmond area for a whole week as stated in his records. "In Virginia, the prospect is very promising. I have preached in two churches and, this morning, am to preach in a third. Rich and poor seem quite ready to hear. Many have been truly awakened."

1787 – 1789 Hampden – Sydney College Revival

- Hampden – Sydney College and Liberty Hall Academy, were the first Presbyterian "Log Colleges" in the South to train ministers for the gospel of Jesus Christ.
- Presbyterian revival broke out at Hampden-Sydney College in 1787, in Prince Edward County, out of a student prayer meeting.
- It gradually extended into counties of Charlotte, Cumberland, Campbell, Bedford east of the Ridge, Rockbridge, and Augusta. "The revival at Hampden-Sydney seems to have begun spontaneously among a small band of students." Two of the students were Cary Allen and William Hull, future great evangelists. President John Blair Smith of the institution, began to meet with the students and encourage them. Soon Hampden-

Sydney became the center of an extensive revival. Many ministers of the gospel were trained here, and they spread the revival spirit throughout the South.
- 1789 Liberty Hall Academy (Current Washington & Lee) Revival
- In 1789 the revival moved westward to Bedford and Rockbridge Counties which became another center of revival.
- Rector William Graham of Liberty Hall Academy and two of his students visited Prince Edward County and Hampden-Sydney in 1789. They carried the revival spirit home. "Lexington now became the center of a revival which extended up and down the Valley of Virginia."
- Liberty Hall Academy in Rockbridge County is now Washington and Lee. Another revival broke out at the Peaks of Otter area in Bedford.

Many ministers were trained under these two college revivals, and each took the Great Awakening revival to their own homes, and then South to NC, SC, GA, and to TN and KY.

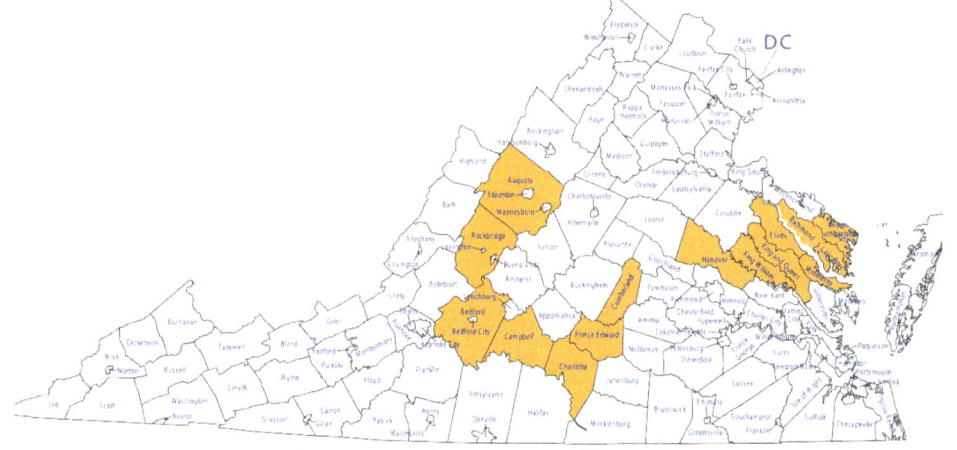

Early Presbyterian Revivals in Virginia

- 1740 – 1758 Centered in Hanover County
- 1787 – 1789 Centered in Hampden – Sydney College
- 1789 Centered in Liberty Hall Academy and Peaks of Otter

Church of England (Anglican)
1763 – 1778 Dinwiddie County plus 29 counties in two states with Rev. Devereux Jarratt.

- Revival started in 1763 with Anglican Priest Devereux Jarratt.
- Jarratt was assigned as Rector of Bath Parish in Dinwiddie County. Included 3 Parishes (Bath, Butterwood, and Sapponey)
- He was evangelical. He had three parishes and soon they all were overflowing. By 1772 the revival had "extended itself in some places for fifty or sixty miles around," to a place called White Oak.
- Soon the revival "extended to a circle of five or six hundred miles east, west, north, and south," with the help of Rector Archibald McRoberts (he died in 1779).
- In 1773, Jarratt started working with the Methodists as a revival was just beginning with them. So itinerant Methodist ministers teamed with Jarratt and reached 29 counties for Christ in two states, Virginia and North Carolina, by 1778. Both used field evangelistic outreaches to reach the people with the message of Christ and his plan of salvation and eternal life in heaven. Many were saved. (See Revival Quotes).
- (Revolutionary War- April 1775 to Sept 1983)

Anglican Reverend Devereux Jarratt (1732 to 1801)
Leader of the Great Awakening in Virginia

A primitive profile on the vestry door of Sapponey Church in Dinwiddie County is believed to portray Devereux Jarratt in his old age. Sapponey Church was one of three churches Jarratt oversaw as rector of Bath Parish." – Encyclopedia Virginia

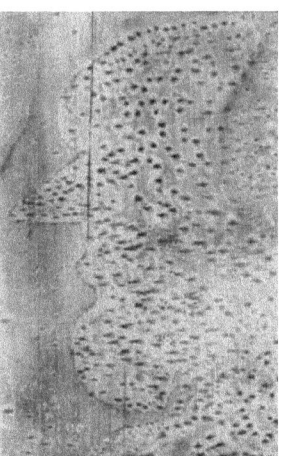

Profile of Devereux Jarratt

- Devereux Jarratt was born in 1732 in New Kent County, VA, the youngest of Robert Jarratt and wife Sarah.
- His father died when he was 6 or 7 years old.
- He received early training by New Lights Presbyterians (evangelical) and was a product of the Great Awakening.
- He had read a book of Whitefield sermons.
- He was an early tutor to school age students, as he loved reading and was self-educated.
- He felt he had a "greater field of usefulness" in the Anglican church, Church of England.
- In 1762, he sailed to England to be ordained on Christmas day. While in England he heard both John Wesley and George Whitefield preach. He arrived back in Yorktown in July 1763.
- On August 19, 1763, Jarratt began his Anglican ministry as rector of Bath Parish in Dinwiddie County. He was 31 years old. The Bath Parish included 3 Parishes (Bath, Butterwood, Sapponey).
- Jarratt was evangelical and an apostle of the Awaking in Virginia.
- He understood the needs of the common people. He stressed religion must be not merely joining a church and confessing a creed. He preached extempore which was very unusual.
- Soon his three parishes were overflowing, and meetings started being held outside.
- Anglican Archibald McRoberts was a co-laborer in the revival as a neighboring rector.
- From the Presbyterians he carried the influences of the Great Awakening to the Anglicans and further encouraged the Methodists, ie. Williams and Walters.
- By 1772, the revival extended 50 to 60 miles around Dinwiddie County.
- Jarratt held open air meetings as the crowds were too large for churches or there was no convenient church.
- Revival widened to 400 to 500 square miles, as an "outpouring of the spirit."
- In 1773, Jarratt's revival merged with the Methodist movement. Early in 1773, Jarratt met Methodist minister Rev. Robert Williams. Williams had arrived in 1772 at Norfolk and Portsmouth.
- Jarratt worked hand in hand with the Methodists.

- Jarratt visited 29 counties in two states, Virginia, and North Carolina. He preached on average 5 sermons a week.
- Jarratt, as an Anglican, was assured that the Methodists had come to build up and not to divide the Church.
- Methodists were evangelical, bringing in ten, fifteen or even 20 converts in a single day. Converts were all ages, all classes, including Black people.
- In 1776, Anglican Priest Rankin was in Virginia, then North Carolina, and back to Virginia. He wrote letters back to England about the revival.
- Jarratt did not like the emotional element of the revival, ie. falling down, tears, drunken in spirit, shouting, voice of joy and gladness. He called it Methodism enthusiasm.
- The Revolutionary War affected the revival. Shadford and Rankin returned to England. John Wesley supported Parliament's right to tax colonists.
- In 1784, there was a breach between Jarratt and the American Episcopal Church.
- What became of Jarratt after the Revolutionary War? He continued preaching at Bath Parish churches. He preached at the Methodist Virginia Conference in Petersburg on June 14, 1790. He continued his close relationship with the Methodists.
- The revival movement in Virginia also affected the Presbyterians, and Baptists. Methodists had spread to every part of the Commonwealth. Jarratt also adopted a centralized organization under Bishops, and an itinerant system to spread the gospel, like the Methodists.
- United Methodist, Baptist, and Presbyterian denominations were flourishing in 1787-88, preaching with and for each other.
- Jarratt died January 29, 1801 at 69 years of age.
- Methodist Rev. Francis Asbury preached Jarratt's funeral on April 19, 1801 at the Bath Parish in Dinwiddie County, Virginia. The two remained close friends, and Jarratt and his wife are mentioned with many visits in Asbury's Journals.

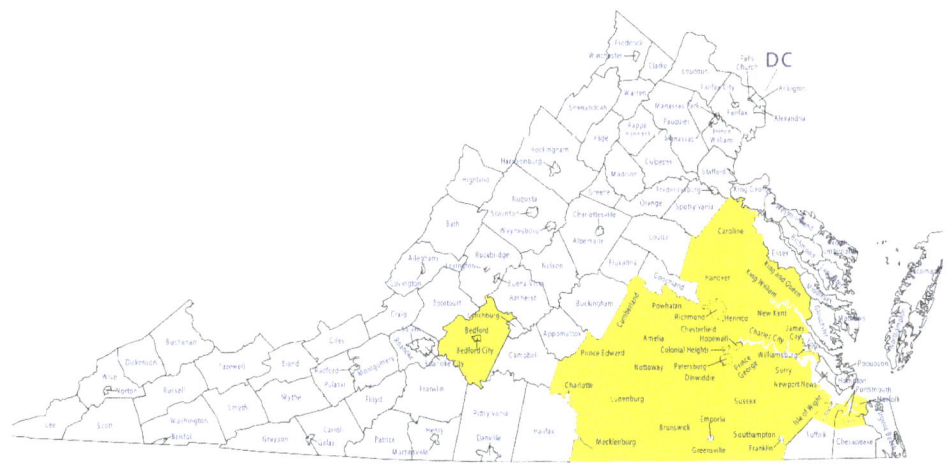

Early Anglican Revival in Virginia

- Anglican Jarratt, Dinwiddie County Revival
- 1763 – 1772; 50 to 60-mile radius around Dinwiddie County
- By 1778 the revival had reached 29 Counties in 2 States (VA and NC), 400 – 500 Square Miles around Dinwiddie with Methodist Itinerants

Methodist
1772 - 1778 Methodist Itinerant ministers with Anglican Rev. Jarratt.
1785 – 1788 Methodist Revival

- When Francis Asbury came to Philadelphia, PA, in 1771, he heard about the Great Awakening in Virginia at a Methodist Conference in Philadelphia. Rev. Robert Williams reported, being the first Methodist minister to visit the Virginia colony early in 1772.
- Asbury wanted to see the Anglican revival in Dinwiddie for himself. He came to Virginia via Norfolk in 1775 and was met by Rev. Robert Williams who gave him an update of the revival. Itinerant Methodist ministers had teamed with Anglican Priest Jarratt and revival spread to 29 counties throughout Virginia and North Carolina, by 1778. (See Revival Quotes.)
- "The revival of 1775-1776 has been designated as the greatest awaking in the history of American Methodism." The unity of the people prepared Virginia for the Revolutionary War.
- The Great Awakening in Virginia continued despite the Revolutionary War (April 1775 to September 1783). The Methodist itinerants fanned revival from Brunswick County to southeastern Virginia in Norfolk, Portsmouth, Nansemond, IOW, Surry, Sussex, etc.
- After the Revolutionary War, in 1785, a "Methodist revival broke out in the southern counties of Virginia, particularly in Brunswick, Sussex, and Amelia circuits." "Blacks and whites were prostrated for hours."
- "Near a thousand souls have been converted in this circuit within a few months."
- "It was not uncommon for people to cease work in the fields in order to hold prayer meetings, and conversions usually followed."
- In Buckingham County, "all three denominations fell heir to revival." "We dwelt together in unity. We preached with and for each other and the Lord again favored the neighborhood with his presence."
- One example was in Sussex Circuit, when a crowd of 5,000 heard the gospel on the first night, "with many more on the second." Preaching to both White and Black people in the open air and in chapel, and in the barn.
- Methodists, through the ordination of lay ministers, made a vast organized missionary evangelistic system for the Lord. "It was nothing for meetings to continue for six or seven hours at a time and last until midnight."
- In Portsmouth in 1788, there were "vast members flocking into the fold of Christ from every quarter. In many places in the circuit as soon as the preacher begins to speak the power of God appears to be present; which is attended with trembling among the people, and falling down; …"

- "the entire area south of the James River from the Blue Ridge to the sea was affected by the Awakening."

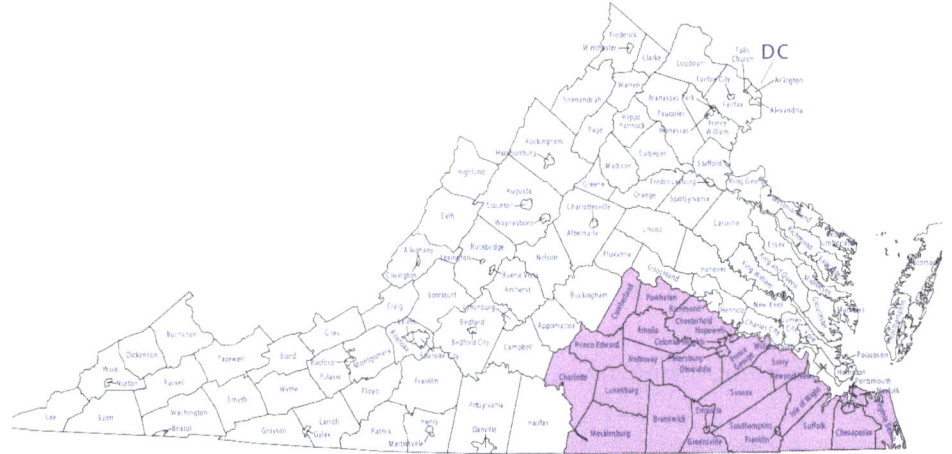
Early Methodist Revivals in Virginia

- 1772 – 1778 with Anglican Jarratt
- 1775 – 1776 First Methodist Revivals
- 1785 – 1788 Centered in Brunswick, Amelia, and Sussex Circuits

Baptist (Separatist)
1755- 1759 From Sandy Creek, NC north to Culpepper, VA

- Baptist revival started at Sandy Creek, North Carolina in 1755, and moved north up the Shenandoah Valley of Virginia to Culpepper in 1759, and in the region of the James River. The Baptist stirred the common folk, advancing "wave after wave of revivals upward from the south."
- "Men like Daniel Marshall and Samuel Harriss traveled far and wide wherever an occasion to preach was within reach, and they became founders of many churches." "Harriss was particularly identified with the revival in the counties north of the James, especially in Culpeper and Orange Counties." "Hundreds of men at times camped on the grounds in order to stay through the meetings and we are told that sometimes the floor would be covered with persons who had been "struck down under conviction of sin."" Harriss suffered much for the gospel at the hands of ruffians.
- The Baptists placed "all authority in the hands of the local churches." The Revival "had in it the fire and fervor of the Whitefield revival." They started singing "a variety of short, violently contrasted verses…" "The one great common doctrine for all Baptists was adult baptism." The Baptists "made sharp attacks on the Established Church with its infant baptism."

1785 – 1789 Northern Neck, VA

- Another Baptist revival started in 1785 in the James River area, in eastern midland and northern Virginia, particularly in the Northern Neck area, and continued until 1789, affecting the whole surrounding area.
- The time of greatest intensity was started by John Leland from 1787 to 1789.
- In an original church in the Upper King and Queen Association, one pastor baptized fifty members in the course of about fifteen days. The following month over sixty were baptized, and then even thirty members monthly.
- "A greater work of grace has probably never been known in Virginia within the limits of one church."
- Large harvests were also reaped in other churches in the Dover Association in the Northern Neck. "It was not unusual to have a larger proportion of a congregation prostrate on the floor; and, in some instances, they lost the use of their limbs. …"
- A united revival started in Prince George County with the Presbyterian, Methodist, and Baptist churches and ministers even sharing pulpits.

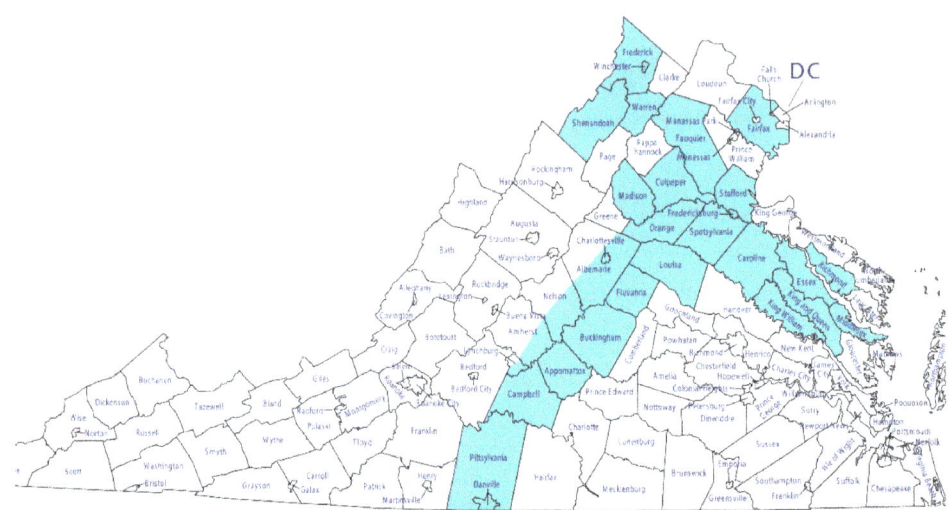

Early Baptist Revival in Virginia

- 1755 – 1759 From Sandy Creek, NC, to Culpepper County (up current Route 29)
- 1785 – 1789 Northern Neck

CAMP MEETINGS

- In 1800, camp meetings started in south central Kentucky, known as the Cumberland country by the Presbyterians. They set the pattern for these outdoor meetings. It was held in Logan County, Kentucky. People were attracted for miles around by the "vivid revivalist preaching of James McGready, who had come from North Carolina.
- In August 1801, the greatest of recorded camp meetings was held at Cane Ridge in Bourbon County, Kentucky. It was planned by Barton W. Stone, a convert of the Hampden-Sydney revival in Virginia. Thousands attended from miles around for ten days. All denominations were invited, and all came. Estimated attendance was 10,000 to 25,000.
- It is said people "saw God face to face," people "fell, wheeled, praised and groaned." "Many falling, jerks, dancing, barking, laughing, running and singing."
- "There was vast confusion and noise, much to the distress of the staid Presbyterian leaders, which led to its repudiation by the Presbyterians."
- "Thereafter it became more and more a Methodist institution and spread rapidly all over the country."
- The first camp meeting in Virginia was in Brunswick County in May of 1803. It started at a new meeting house, which afterwards was called Camp Meeting House.
- The camp meetings were a locally controlled institution.
- Stith Mead was one of the most affected Virginia camp meeting organizers. He was especially active in Bedford, Campbell, and Amherst Counties. He was termed as the "father of the Virginia camp meeting."
- In 1804, Lorenzo Dow, a free-lance evangelist, came to Virginia and teamed with Mead.
- Camp Meetings were often held as a one to two day extension of the Quarterly Methodists Conferences when open to preachers and local members, and were called "love feasts."
- "Camp Meetings did represent an important progression in the Methodist program to evangelize the nation."
- In 1811 Asbury wrote to Thomas Coke "that the church held four hundred camp meetings annually and could claim to "congregate, possibly, three millions.""

"By 1812 Bishop Asbury recorded in his *Journal* that at least 400 camp meetings would be held that year under Methodist auspices, and it was probable that at least 1,000 Methodist camp meetings were being conducted throughout the country by the year 1820. Bishop Asbury characterized the camp meeting as Methodist harvest-time." A few documented camp meetings included:

- 1805, September and October at Ebenezer, where 1700 attended.
  Edge of Franklin County, held a multitude in wilderness country, "100 tents, 60 wagons, besides carriages."
  New Kent County
  Popular Spring Church
  Pace's Meeting House

Cole's Chapel
- 1807, Powhatan County, October 12, 1807 "the Lord came down."
- 1808, Near Portsmouth at Taylor's, June 9-13, 1808.
- 1812, Providence Meeting House near Williamsburg in New Kent County.

Quotes from the Great Awakening of Virginia Revivals

1775 "shaking among the dry bones" which "increased from week to week" "sometimes ten to twelve have been deeply converted of sin in one day…Numbers of old-and gray headed, of middle-aged persons, of youth age, of little children, were the subjects of this work" "outpouring of the Spirit" in an area of 400 - 500 square miles in circumstance of Dinwiddie. "power of the Lord came down upon the assembly like a rushing wind." Note 1.

"Recorded crowds of 2,000 to 3,000. A model for Methodist expansion for 40 years."

1775 Robert Williams, first Methodist preacher to visit the colony, carried the revival news to Francis Asbury on his arrival in Norfolk April 1775. From Asbury's Journal, "I met with Brother Williams from Virginia, who gave me a great account of the work of God in these parts—five or six hundred souls justified by faith, and five or six circuits formed." Note 2, P. 145.

1775 "Methodism began as a revival within the Anglican Church in America, as well as in England." Note 2 P. 145 from Jarratt's Autobiography.

1775 Anglican Thomas Rankin of England, on a preaching tour of Southern Virginia and North Carolina wrote, "In both colonies the chapels overflowed with the large congregations and outdoor meetings had to be arranged." "I scarce ever remember such a season. No chapel or preaching in Virginia would have contained one third of the congregation." Everywhere on the circuit both Black and White people were eager for the gospel and Rankin tells us that he was "preached" almost to the point of exhaustion. The same must have been true of Jarratt, also. Note 2. P.148.

1776 " ..when such power descended, that hundreds fell to the ground, and the house seemed to shake with the presence of God. The chapel was full of white and black, and many were without that could not get in." "…faces bathed in tears… My voice was drowned amidst the groans and prayers of the congregation." Note 3.

1776 Jesse Lee said, "the greatest revival of religion I have ever seen." Note 2. P 149

1787 Many were overwhelmed with emotion and broke out in loud praises to God, while others wept and praised the Lord with all their might." Hundreds "were so overcome with the power of God that they fell down, and lay on the floor or on the ground." Note 4.

"..first day no less than 5,000 were present and the second day twice that number," at an open air meeting in Sussex.

1804 "… there was a huge gathering in Suffolk, south of the lower James River. A zealot in the work of revival reported that it had been "a camp-meeting" and had begun "on Friday and continued day and night without intermission till Monday evening." During that time there had been "upwards of four hundred souls, including the blacks… powerfully converted to God." "… many fell to the ground and cried for mercy,.." Meeting was at Smith's Mill and led by Daniel Hall, a Methodist evangelist. Note 5.

1827 Camp Meeting on Williams Farm in Suffolk, at the fork of Pitchkettle Road and Murphy's Mill Road. "Hundreds were converted, and Providence [Methodist] Church was established as an outgrowth of this camp meeting." Note 6.

1865 In August, "a gracious revival commenced and continued for nineteen days and nights, with the conversion of 77 persons, 25 united with the Suffolk Christian Church, and others uniting with Christian Churches in the county or with other denominations." This was after the church was closed for two years for the Civil War. The pastor was Dr. W.B. Wellons, who was assisted by Rev. James Munoy of the Presbyterian Church, and the Methodist. Note 7.

Note 1. Sweet, William, "Virginia Methodism", p 67. From Francis Asbury Journal Vol I., 208-224
Note 2. Gewehr, Wesley M. "The Great Awakening in Virginia (1740-1790)
Note 3. Isaac, Rhys, "The Transformation of Virginia 1740-1790" p.261. Contents from Anglican Thomas Rankin letter to John Wesley, on his visit to Virginia.
Note 4. Sweet, William "Virginia Methodism"   p 122
Note 5. Isaac, Rhys, "The Transformation of Virginia" p 316
Note 6. Providence UMC Church History
Note 7. Suffolk Christian Church History

Results of the Great Awakening in Virginia, 1740 to 1790

- United Anglicans, Presbyterians, Methodists, and Baptists in revival.
- Freedom from denominational bias.
- Estimated 50,000 conversions.
- Evangelicals regarded God as the sole head of the Church.
- Accustomed people into self-government in their religious habits.
- Welded the common people into a democracy.
- Revivalists were first to weld together plain people to bring them to the realization of their strength.
- Led away from special privileges of the Established Church (Church of England), maintained by taxation and compulsory payment to tithe to the Anglican Church.
- Religious Freedom.
    1. Presbyterians. Controlled by elders and pastors. Divided by Synods. Congregations' right to choose their pastors.
    2. Methodists. Centralized with Bishops and Conferences. Bishop assigned preachers.
    3. Baptists. Independent churches, with associations. Churches called their own pastors.

- Suspended salaries of Anglican clergy and the support of state religion after the Revolutionary War.
- Protestant Episcopal Church created.
- "Undoubtedly the Great Awakening was one of the great contributing factors in the development of democracy in Virginia."
- The Great Awakening gave a strong impetus to both ministerial and secular education in Virginia.
- The Great Awakening brought about a change in attitude toward slavery.
- Education of Black people.
- Great revivals in Virginia drew many slaveholders into the church.
- Created a social revolution with new values, concerning drunkenness, swearing, dress code, playing cards and dice, dancing, etc..
- Great Awakening was primarily a revival of personal religion. ….. made for the betterment of society.
- The Great Awakening gave us songs and melodies of the Moravians, and the hymns of the Wesleys.
- Several sources of Great Awakening in Middle Colonies:
    1. Revival from Germantown, PA in 1722 among the German/Dutch Reformers.
    2. Establishment in 1726 of Log College for training ministers.
    3. Early Log College graduates in 1729 and 1732 led revivals.
    4. Beginning revival among Presbyterians in 1734 in New England by Jonathan Edwards.
    5. The establishment of the "Holy Club" at Oxford, England and the coming of Methodist itinerant evangelists in 1739.
    6. The Great Awakening in 1740, in New England, led by Jonathan Edwards.

George Whitefield's revival spirit as a Methodist working with German/Dutch Reformers, Methodists, Presbyterians, and Baptists denominations was key. He partnered with Jonathan Edwards throughout New England. Whitefield's written sermons were also a source of revivals. Everywhere he preached in his seven trips to America, including his five visits to Virginia, there was a revival spirit and huge crowds, some as high as 30,000.

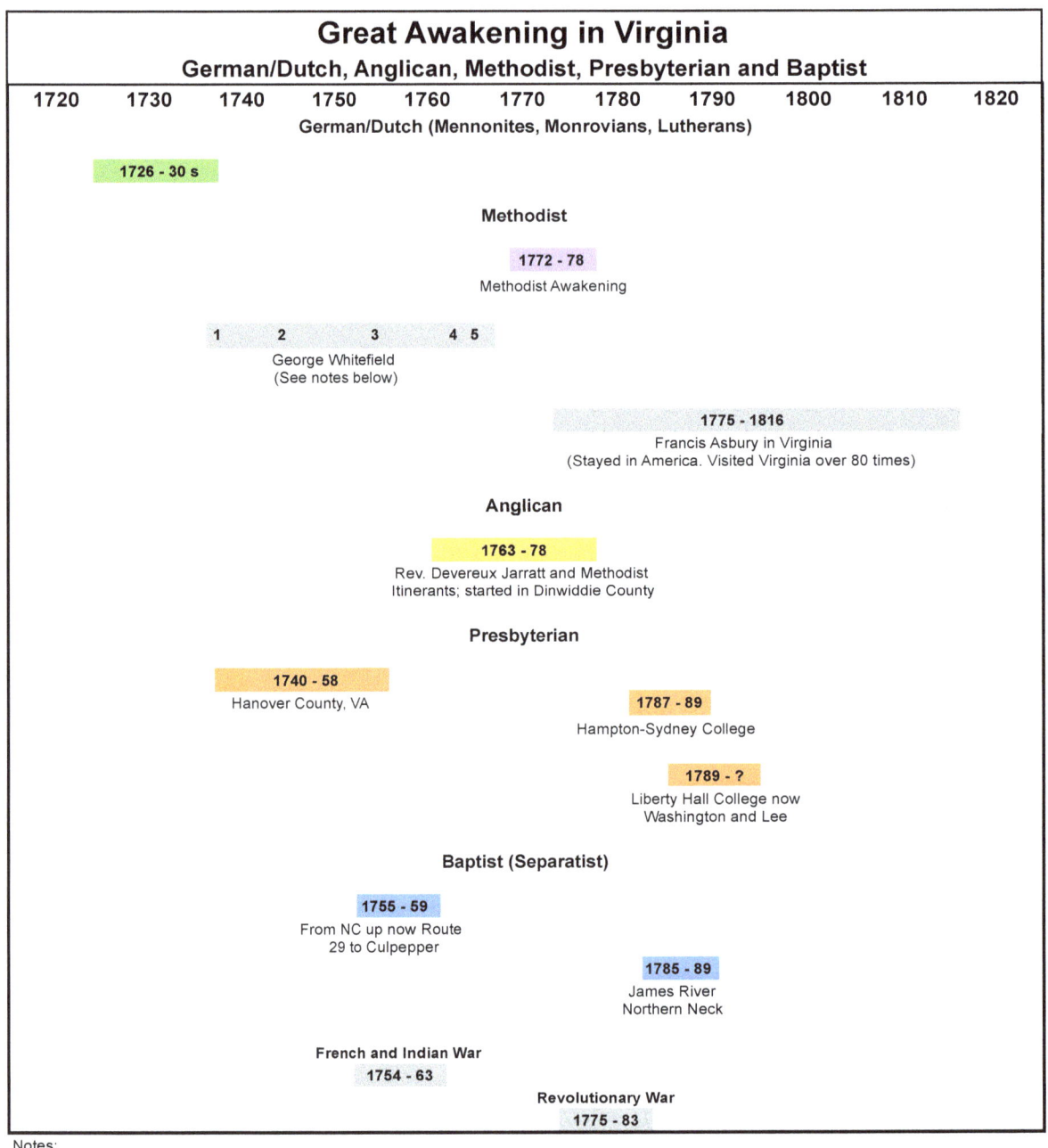

Notes:
1. Dec 15-16, 1739 Williamsburg and Plantations. Preached Bruton Parish
2. Oct 14-18, 1745 Hanover County
3. Jan 1755 Richmond area, one week revitalizing Presbyterian revival
4. Aug 24, 1763 Northern Neck
5. Apr 1765 Petersburg. Met with Patrick Henry

PART V

Rekindling the Flames of Revival

"There are the places where the Spirit of God has come, and heaven and earth have become very close, "Thin Places."

Chuck D. Pierce *

* "There are the places where the Spirit of God has come, and heaven and earth have become very close, 'Thin Places.'" "As we move into a new year, the church is entering a season of war and triumph." - Chuck D. Pierce, president of Glory of Zion, Zion International Ministries, and vice-president of Global Harvest Ministries, Article "Happy New Era," Charisma Magazine December 2019.

REKINDLE THE FLAMES OF REVIVAL

The Great Awakening in Virginia during the 1700s has been documented in our State's history and in the church history of our State's Protestant denominations; Church of England (Episcopal), Presbyterians, Reformers, Methodists, and Baptists.

Many were saved and professed Jesus Christ as Savior and Lord as the result of the Awakening. Many churches were started in all the denominations, and then greatly increased in size and in influence.

The unity that revival brought about in the denominations prepared the Christians for the Revolutionary War. It happened once; it can happen again. It is up to the Body of Christ in Virginia to believe for another revival in the Church of Jesus Christ in our great State. God wants to do something new in His church. God wants to save souls for His Kingdom before He returns for His Church.

Matthew 16: 18-19 states, "I will build My church, and the gates of hell will not overpower it. I will give you the keys of the kingdom of heaven: whatever you bind on earth will be bound in heaven, and whatever you loose on earth will be loose in heaven." That is a powerful church, bearing much fruit.

The Body of Christ has become too complacent, stagnate, and set in its own rituals and works. Preaching a watered down, formal gospel, without the power and gifts of the Holy Spirit, and without signs and wonders. There is false teaching and sin in the church that has not been rooted out nor confessed.

There is no evangelism, no burden for reaching the unsaved, no discipleship training for the converted, and the message of the gospel of Jesus Christ has no meaning. The church is comfortable where they are. There is no vision for their city, nor seeing their communities as their mission field and their responsibility in the Kingdom of God.

Proverbs 29:18 tells us that, "Where there is no vision, the people perish."

The church is silent.

How is America to survive without moral convictions, if the church has none? The onslaught of issues of abortion, gay marriage, homosexually, gender identity, pornography, online media without constraints, run away national debt for our children to bear, and many more issues which are against the teachings of the Bible and the Ten Commandments.

Virginia and all of America need REVIVAL. The Commonwealth of Virginia was founded as a Christian Colony, and later became the basis for the governmental foundations of our nation,

America. Both were based on the Christian principles and based on the Word of God, the Holy Bible. Bring us back to our roots, Lord. Revive us again Lord, with Thy Love.

Virginia was the first in God's eyes and purpose in fulfilling God's plan to reach the Native Americans and spread the Gospel in this new world. Virginia is the Eastern Gate to America, for Jesus Christ and the message of the Bible. Virginia has a big responsibility in the future of America.

What can we do?

THE BODY OF CHRIST

As Individuals

"Jesus said, 'If two of you agree on earth concerning anything that they ask, it will be done for them by My Father in heaven.'"
MATTHEW 18:19

Remember
- Remember how God used the Church of England (COE) to bring the Gospel of Jesus Christ to Virginia. "Virginia" being almost all of present America at that time, per the 1606 Charter.
- Remember how God used the COE to establish the first permanent settlement in America.
- Remember how God used the COE to establish our governmental democracy based on Biblical truths.
- Remember how all the various denominations were started as part of The Protestant Reformation process.
- In Deuteronomy chapters 6,7, and 8, God told the Israelites to always remember His mighty deeds and to tell their children for generations to come.

Repent
- Repent and confess our sins of forgetting what God has done in the past through Virginia.
- Romans 3:23 - *"for all have sinned and fall short of the Glory of God."*
- 1 John 1:9 - *"If we confess our sins, he is faithful and just and will forgive us our sins.."*
- 2 Corinthians 7:10 - *"Godly sorrow brings repentance that leads to salvation and leaves no regret,…"*

Rebirth
- Be reborn in Jesus Christ and become a new creation in Christ who forgets all our sins, and gives us eternal hope and a future. Lord let sorrow turn to Joy.

- John 3:16 - *"For God so loved the world that he gave his only begotten Son, that whosoever believeth in him should not perish but have everlasting life."*

As a Collective Church and Region

Prayer: *Lord make Virginia the center of revival again. May the Church rise up and become a pillar of truth, a winner of souls, a light in the community and the world, and a center of great works.*

Rekindle
- Rekindle our love for the Lord and for others. Also rekindle the burden for the lost and the unsaved without Christ.
- Refire the flames of revival that were first stirred in Virginia in the 1700's Awakening.
- Then pray for the flames of revival in Virginia to be reignited and spread throughout our State.

Rejoice
- Express joy or gladness for what God has done and will do again. Sing unto the Lord!
- Philippians 4:4 - *"Rejoice in the Lord always. I will say it again: Rejoice!"*
- There is power in praise which leads to worship.

Revival
- Revival of Body, Soul, and Spirit.
- Acts 2: 1-4 - *"When the day of Pentecost came, they were all together in one place. Suddenly a sound like the blowing of a violent wind came from heaven and filled the whole house where they were sitting. They saw what seemed to be tongues of fire that separated and came to rest on each of them. All of them were filled with the Holy Spirit....."*
- Acts 2:47 - *"Day by day the Lord added to their numbers those who were being saved."*

Reconnect
- In John 13:34-35 - *"Jesus said, 'A new command I give you: Love one another. As I have loved you, so you must love one another. By this all men will know that you are my disciples if you love one another.'"*
- Reconnect with brothers and sisters in the local Body of Christ of your city or town. Join with other denominations who have a burden for the area, to meet the spiritual and physical needs locally.
- Reach out.
- Remember there is power in unity.

Rebuild
- Rebuild together as His army of warriors in the Body of Christ. First individually, then our families; our churches, through triumph and winning the lost; our communities, through churches meeting the needs; our State; and our Nation.
- Stand firm together and take back Virginia for the Lord.
- Rebuild our State of Virginia to God's vision for our State.

Reformation – back to the beginning
- The dictionary defines *Reform* as "improved or corrected as in behavior or morals, or made better by the removal of errors, abuses, etc."
- Lord, reform our thinking to recognize all God's creatures are created equally. Body of Christ, may we see ourselves as one in Christ Jesus.
- Galatians 3: 26-28 - *"You are all sons of God through faith in Christ Jesus, for all of you who were baptized into Christ have clothed yourselves with Christ. There is neither Jew nor Greek, slave nor free, male nor female, for you are all one in Christ Jesus."*
- Revelation 5:9 - *"and they sang a new song: … from every tribe and language and people and nation."*

Rapture Ready
- Be ready to meet the Lord when He returns.
- 1 Thessalonians 4:16-17 - *"For the Lord himself shall descend from heaven with a shout, with the voice of the archangel, and with the trump of God: and the dead in Christ shall rise first. Then we which are alive and remain shall be caught up together with them in the clouds, to meet the Lord in the air: and so shall we ever be with the Lord."*

A Call to Prayer and Fasting for the State of Virginia

"As Virginia goes, so goes the Nation"
- Prophecy

Virginia Has Been Called:

Birthplace of our Nation
Cradle of our Nation
Womb of our Nation
Birthplace of the Church of Jesus Christ in our Nation, (First Protestant Church in America)
Seedbed of America

Believe and Pray together for Revival. There is power in agreement!
Will you join us?
Will you organize a group in your church to pray?
Will you be a part of a community action group?
Go to www.RekindleVA.com to answer the call. The web site has much information and timely updates, and local like- minded contacts in your area.

Mission: Rekindle Flames of Revival in Virginia

To Rekindle the flames of revival in the State of Virginia through researching past revivals, sharing of faith founders portraits of early Protestant denominational evangelists that promoted revival of the church in Virginia, through the salvation message of Jesus Christ based on the Bible, and personal repentance of sin. To promote unity and love of the denominations, and to stir up the Body of Christ for another Great Awakening in Virginia. Acts 2:1-4 says, *"When the day of Pentecost came, they were all together in one place. Suddenly a sound like the blowing of a violent wind came from heaven and filled the whole house where they were sitting. They saw what seemed to be tongues of fire that separated and came to rest on each of them. All of them were filled with the Holy Spirit..."*

Proposed Actions:

1. To provide research of God's plan to evangelize the Native Americans, the Indians, the First Nation People of America.
2. To provide research and background of the various early Protestant denominations that evangelized Virginia.
3. To provide research of early Great Awakenings of God's spirit, revivals, in Virginia.
4. To create an excitement of what He did in the past, and can do again, in Virginia.
5. To promote statewide prayer for revival in Virginia.
6. To develop and provide a book of early Protestant vision, ministry, and revivals in Virginia, the eastern gate of America.
7. To develop and distribute a short video for Rekindle Virginia.
8. To develop a web site and flyers for Rekindle.
9. To adopt and highlight the hymn, "Revive Us Again," as the theme song for this mission.
10. The story is not over. Remember, Repent, Rebirth, Rekindle, Rejoice, Revival, Reconnect, Rebuild, Reform, and Rapture Ready.

About the hymn "Revive Us Again"

Verse 4

Revive Us Again-
fill each heart with Thy love;
May each soul be rekindled
with fire from above.

Chorus
Hallelujah, Thine the glory!
Hallelujah, amen!
Hallelujah, Thine the Glory!
Revive us again.

- Words written by William Paton Mackay, (1839-1885) or 1888?
- Educated at University of Edinburgh, Scotland.
- Medical Doctor
- Revival in Scotland in 1859-60 with Charles Finney and others.
- Revival movement produced many hymns.
- Hymn written in 1863 or 1867, based on Psalm 85:6 and Habakkuk 3:2.
- Ordained Presbyterian Minister
- Became Presbyterian Minister at Prospect Street Presbyterian Church, Hull, Scotland in 1868, until death in an accident.
- Wrote 17 hymns.
- Music by John J. Husband 1815.
- Public Domain

References

Alley, Reuben Edward, "The History of Baptist in Virginia", published by Virginia Baptist General Board.
Andrews, Kenneth R. "Trade, Plunder, and Settlement", 1984
Bewes, Richard. "Wesley Country". 2003
Billings, Warren M. "Jamestown and the Founding of the Nation", ?
Caknipe, John, Jr. "Southside Virginia Chronicles". 2014
"Chuckatuck Crossroads in Time", 2011
Christian History Magazine, Francis Asbury, Pioneer of Methodism, Issue 114
Christian History Magazine, The Wesley's, Issue 69
Christian History Magazine, The American Puritans. Issue 41
Christian History Magazine, Camp Meetings & Circuit Riders. Issue 45
Christian History Magazine, Luther leads the Way. Issue 115
Christian History Magazine, John Calvin. Volume V, No 4
Christian History Magazine, Moravians. Issue 9
Christian History Magazine, Building the City of God, Issue 94
Christian History Magazine, Richard Baxter and the English Puritans, Issue 89
Christian History Magazine, Baptist, Issue 126
Comfort, Ray, "Susanna Wesley Her Remarkable Life". 2014
Clark, Elmer T. editor. "The Journal and Letters of Francis Asbury" Vol I, 1771 to 1793. 1958
Clark, Elmer T. editor. "The Journal and Letters of Francis Asbury" Vol II, 1794 to 1816. 1958
Clark, Elmer T. editor. "The Journal and Letters of Francis Asbury" Vol III, The Letters. 1958
Dallimore, Arnold A., "Susanna Wesley"1993
Eisenberg, William Edward. " The Lutheran Church in Virginia 1717-1962, 1967
Foote, William Henry. "Sketches of Virginia" 1856
Gewehr, Wesley M. "The Great Awakening in Virginia, 1740-1790" 1930
Gyertson, David J. Dr. "God's Work Stands", Regent University,
Hagermann, James. "The Heritage of Virginia", 1986, 1988
Haile, Edward Wright, "John Smith in the Chesapeake", 2008
Hansford, Thelma. "Churches in York County", 1972
Hatch, Charles E. Jr. "The First Seventeen Years Virginia (1607-1624)", 1957
Hobbs, Kermit and Paquette, William A. "Suffolk, A Pictorial History", 1987

Isaac, Rhys. "The Transformation of Virginia 1740-1790", 1982

Jarratt, Devereux. "The Life of the Reverend Devereux Jarratt". 1806

Kidd, Thomas S. "George Whitefield America's Spiritual Founding Father".2014

Knight, John R. "The Cape Henry Threshold"., 1990

Mapp, Alf J. "The Virginia Experiment", 1957

Marsden, J.B. "The History of the Early Puritans", 1955

Mason, George Carrington. "Colonial Churches of Tidewater Virginia", 1945

Maxson, Charles Hartshorn. "The Great Awakening in the Middle Colonies".1920

McCary, Ben C. "Indians in Seventeenth-Century Virginia",

Miller, Basil. "John Wesley",

Moore, Matthew H., "Sketches of Pioneers of Methodism in North Carolina and Virginia", 1884

Morison, Samuel Eliot. "The European Discovery of America, The Northern Voyages 500-1600". 1971.

Morison, Samuel Eliot. "The European Discovery of America, The Southern Voyages 1492-1616". 1974.

Nelson, John K. "A Blessed Company", 2001

Nygaard, Norman E., "Bishop on Horseback, The Story of Francis Asbury", 1962

Packer, J.I."A Quest for Godliness The Puritan Vision of the Christian Life". 1990

Paine, Robert. "Life and Times of William McKendree Bishop of the Methodist Episcopal Church",1922

Parramore, Thomas C. "Norfolk, The First Four Centuries", 1994

Patriot Prints. "The Charters of Virginia" 1994

Perry, Richard L. edited by. "Sources of our Liberties". 1991

Providence Foundation, "Jamestown 400th Anniversary, The Role of Faith in Founding of the Nation"

Quinn, David B, and Quinn, editors. "The First Colonists (1584-1590)", 1982 Documents on the Planting of the First English Settlement in North America. Introduction on Richard Hakluyt.

Rountree, Helen. "Pocahontas's People". 1990

Rouse, Parke, Jr, "Spanish Ahead of English in Virginia", Daily Press Newspaper

Sweet, William Warren. "Virginia Methodism" MCMLV

"The Five Great Documents of Liberty" for Henricus College (1619)

"The River Binds Us", 2007

Vaughan, Alden T. Edited by. "The Puritan Tradition in America (1620-1730)", 1972

Wayland, John W. "Germanna Outpost of Adventure 1714 – 1956", 1989

Wigger, John. "American Saint, Francis Asbury and the Methodists", 2009

Worrall, Jay, Jr. "The Friendly Virginians (Quakers)", 1994

About Dorothy "Dot" L. Dalton

Born and raised in eastern Ohio
Graduated with a BS in Mathematics from Ohio University
Founder and Former President, IMPACT SUFFOLK in Virginia
Former President of the Board for a Nansemond Indian project, Mattanock Town
Former Advisory Board member to a local community bank
Former State of Virginia Coordinator for Native American Resource Network
Co-Founder of Virginia Prayer Network, praying for governmental leaders
Former Coordinator for Eastern Virginia Lydia intercessory prayer network
Retired Computer Consultant
Former Director of Customer Support for a Computer Software company
Former GS 14 Program Manager with U.S. Navy information systems command
Widow, Married to Clem Edward Dalton, Retired U.S. Naval Officer

Milton Keynes UK
Ingram Content Group UK Ltd.
UKHW020731260324
440001UK00006B/49

9 780578 816814